Secret Society
of the Shamans

Secret Society of the Shamans

"Mystery Religions" of the North American Indians Revealed

Global Communications

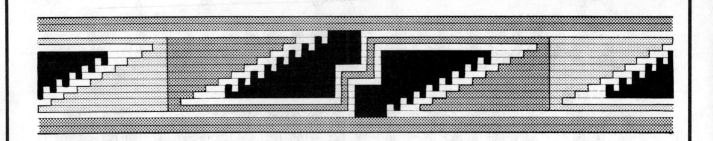

Editorial & Art Direction:
Timothy Green Beckley
Typography by:
Cross-Country Consultants

For foreign and reprint rights, contact:
Rights Department
Global Communications
P.O. Box 753, New Brunswick, NJ 08903

ISBN: 0-938294-44-X

Special Credit:
Front and back cover art copyright © by
Timotao Ikoshy Montoya.

Contents

About The Author

Dennis Morrison has been writing historical non-fiction since the late 1960's. His interests turned to Indian heritage eight years ago when he and his wife began doing extensive excavations of a Late Woodland village site in his own backyard. As a freelance author, Dennis has published over 300 articles pertaining to history and pre-history, as well as publishing many historical booklets. Dennis' interest in religions and myths of Native Americans began with his discovery of a mysterious Indian image stone. This, Dennis' first book, includes the story of that unusual stone that still remains an enigma.

Author Dennis M. Morrison, on Black Rock in Greenbush, on the Shore of Lake Huron. Black Rock has been an Indian Ceremonial Spot for centuries and is one of those special places where the monitors dwell.   Photo by Kathy W. Morrison

DEDICATED

This book is dedicated to my friend and mentor: Jerry Wagner.
Not long before your passing you said we would have a chance to write together—
Now I feel we have.

4

Chapter One:
The Midaywiwin:
Society of Secrets

It seems as though mankind stumbles across the mysteries of the ancients usually quite by accident. My discovery of the Midaywiwin or the Grand Medicine Society was on just such a note.

My main interest in prehistory had been, for many years, the relics laying concealed beneath the mat of rotted leaves here in northeast Michigan. All that changed one hot August afternoon as my wife Kathy, son Mikie and I made a couple of very nice and unusual discoveries.

For eight years now we have been digging a site called Old Van Etten Creek. It is located in a wonderfully peaceful woodland setting about a ½ mile from downtown Oscoda, Michigan.

That this little green gem even exists unspoiled by the ravages of encroaching civilization is in itself a miracle. It is about a three block long piece of land, equally as deep, bordering on the banks of Van Etten Creek. To the north, having obliterated a good portion of this Late Woodland Indian occupa-

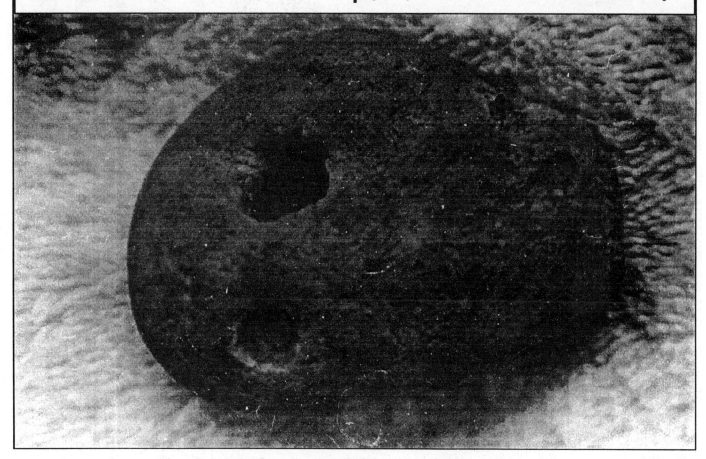

Reverse side of the "star burst" Miday-related stone. Its unique appearance of a human skull cannot be denied.

tion site (700 AD), is a large housing development. The scenario to the south is the same. How long the great Manitouls that these ancients worshiped will protect this little portal of time is yet to be seen. For all our sakes I hope it is forever.

As you walk into this prehistoric village you will find that the ground is on three levels, each reflecting higher water tables in the past. The highest level is the oldest dating back over 2,000 years. I called this a portal of time and sometimes I feel this is true, for the relics never seem to run out. Seldom do we ever enter this site that we don't come out with a bucket of pottery shards and many stone tools. In fact from the small area that remains of Old Van Etten Creek we have recovered the remains of close to 500 prehistoric pottery vessels—a phenomenal number for an area this size.

When I say the remains of pottery vessels I mean that we find shards or pieces of them, but rarely ever complete pots. Of course there is good reason for this, over a millennium of freeze thaw cycles have smashed earthenware vessels into pieces. We are able to approximately date the site, and tell how many vessels were present by the rim shards which are quite distinctive.

This particular day was quite stifling. The humidity made it seem as though we were breathing water. Merely walking on such a day is an effort, but some force had beckoned me, lead me to forget the discomforts of the flesh and conduct excavations. Walking into the woods we heard the monotonous drone of what must have been a million mosquitoes. They generally bother us quite a bit when digging, but this day for some reason they kept their distance. Perhaps the hand of Gitchi Manitou the Great Spirit was upon us—or maybe it was just to darned hot for them too!

We picked out a somewhat shaded spot and with shovel in hand I penetrated into mother earth—she gave not a wince at my intrusion. Gently I made a circular cut in the black earth and then as opening a doorway into another era and culture I peeled the decomposition of centuries away.

I gave a slight gasp for laying before us were seventeen small pottery shards. I could tell by the decoration that they were all from the same vessel. We

Tiny child's vessel found with the Miday inscribed "star burst" stone. The little pot is 2½ inches tall by 2½ inches across.

carefully removed the shards and placed them in a baggie. In doing this I fitted enough together to tell that most of the pot was there, making it the most complete vessel we had ever found. Later we would wash it and reassemble what nature had torn asunder.

When pieced together we found the pot to be a child's vessel about two inches tall and two inches across. It is bell shaped and has very nice incised geometric designs, also it was about 90% complete.

Had this been the only find that day I would have been delighted, but the most unusual was yet to come. We were digging on the edge of a hearth (campfire). This was attested to by the waxy black loam and the plethora of bones. Digging on down below the charred bones I found an artifact that would prove to be a link between my Old Van Etten Creek Site and the Midaywiwin, a secret society of Great Lakes Indians.

I gave another gasp as I uncovered a palm sized stone with a large hole in the center of it. The hole immediately made the stone suspect to me and I thought first of a pendant. This turned out to be the case.

The stone was covered with sand and as I brushed that off I became more excited, for here was not just a pendant but one with an incised design. The pendant has two faces, first I will describe what I consider to be the front.

The Pendant is of a light weight stone and is tan colored. The hole appears to be a natural formation, however, it had been scraped out and enlarged. The scrapping marks are quite apparent. The hole appears to be "counter sunk" being larger in the front and tapering towards the back. Radiating out from the hole in a sort of "star burst" pattern are incised lines. Half of these straight lines are circumvented by a circular line traveling through them.

The back of the stone is just as unusual though it has no incised designs. The back is a little eerie looking very much resembles a human skull. The natural hole comes all the way through, next to it is a second hole made with a stone drill. This gives the appearance of two eyes. There is another drilled hole where the mouth would be. The drilled holes do not go all the way through. Given these holes and the general countenance of the stone you have a look very similar to a skull.

I became obsessed with this particular find as it was so unusual. The reason it is so unusual is that, yes we find abstract designs incised into pottery, but

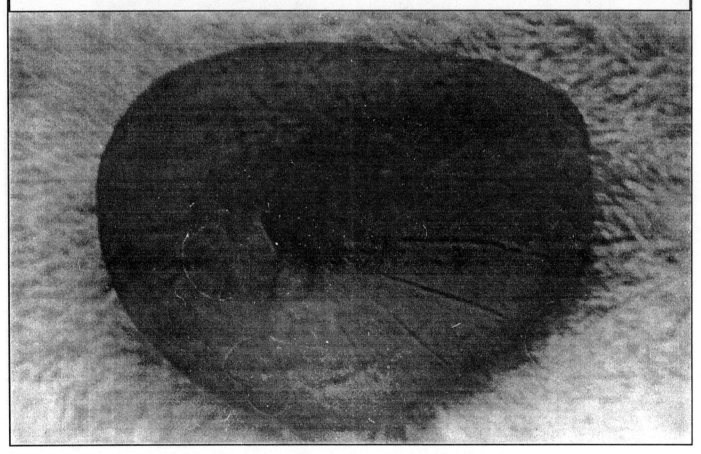

never anything in stone! This was not just an abstract design either, this was a familiar design. My task then was to track down where I had seen it before.

I had seen the design in a book titled, *Indian Rock Paintings of the Great Lakes,* by Selwyn Dewdney and Kenneth E. Kidd (University of Toronto/1973). In this book was a drawing of a birch bark scroll with pictographs on it. These scrolls were used by the Midaywiwin and are the closest thing to native writing found north of Mexico. There upon that scroll was the same "star burst" design, just as I had remembered seeing it.

Here was a connection between my village site and this ultra secret Indian healing/shaman society. I began a detailed investigation into the Midaywiwin. My investigation gave me a unique insight into the people who lived at my Late Woodland village complex. Whereas archaeology only uncovers the cold scientific facts at a site, this connection brought with it a cornucopia of oral and written tradition that brought these villagers to life for me.

The birch scrolls were sacred indeed. Some that still exist are of great antiquity and can not be deciphered. The information contained in these scrolls was revealed only to select Indians. Rarely did whites get a glimpse of the Miday. The six foot scrolls were a combined text book and prayer book, that gave directions for initiation rites and other sacred rituals.

The Secret Society, the Midaywiwin, is said to have been given to the Indians by Manabozho also less familiarly called Wiskendjac. In the Anishinabe or Chippewa religious tradition, Manabozho was second only to the Great Spirit—Gitchi Manitou. In the mythology of these ancient peoples whose very name, Anishinabe, means "original man,"—Manabozho was a helper in creation to Gitchi Manitou. It was Manabozho who in times past was the great protector of the Anishinabe and who obtained the Midaywiwin for their exclusive benefit.

Until recent years, anthropologists including Harold Hickson placed the origin of the Midaywi-

win in the 17th century. We now know that this is erroneous, that in fact through discoveries such as my inscribed pendant and the stone discs of chapter two, that its origins find their roots hundreds, perhaps thousands of years before the first Europeans came to America. It was during the 17th century onward that the true Midaywiwin became diluted with ideas brought in by the European mind.

The Miday priest wore a bonnet of many different feathers so to speak. Through him was preserved the folk history and traditions of the tribe. By the use of birch bark scrolls he also preserved the knowledge of medicinal plants used for healing the infirmities of "his" people. For him, and on rare occasion her, the secret to long life and good health was to have near spotless personal conduct, as well as having a good knowledge of the proper use of herbs and music. Herbs and music combined together, merged in a magical metamorphosis which amplified both of their healing properties.

The Grand Medicine Society had its restrictions that were placed on the priests. In fact, in some ways the Midaywiwin sounds much like the secret societies of today. For example the Midaywiwin had a limited membership. It worked in a stepped manner, that is to say that there were at least four differ-

ent levels to be attained. Some sources claim there were as many as eight degrees!

Each degree had to be attained in progression and necessitated mastering certain sacred knowledge as well as in some cases a hefty financial sacrifice.

The first degree Miday priest was required to possess a knowledge of a few common herbs and the music that made them work. These things were kept in his miday bag, not unlike a medicine bag.

Higher degrees were taught the great mysteries of the society. According to Jefferson Danziger Jrl., *Chippewas of the Lake Superior,* these higher ranks were taught the properties of the rare herbs and even the nature of vegetable poisons. Songs used in rituals as well as other instructions were recorded on the birch bark Miday scrolls that had pictures engraved on them suggesting the ideas to be remembered through the generations.

Regular meetings of the society are held in the spring and summer in a lodge called the Midewigan. Only members were allowed in the Midewigan, and before initiates could be admitted they had to fulfill a period of purification.

An excellent description of the Midaywiwin and Midewigan was written in 1852 by Warren. You must remember in this account that some of the

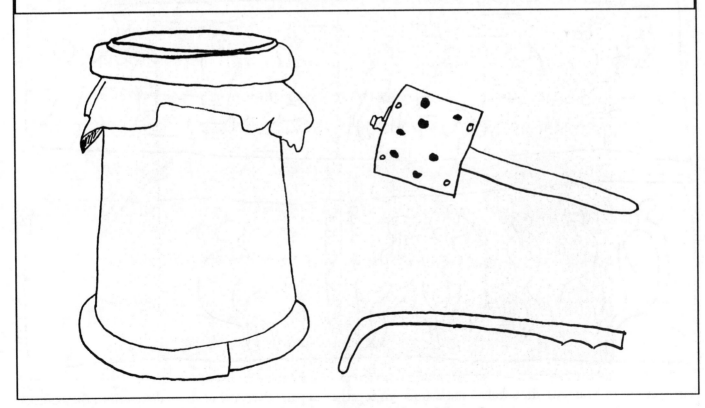

Midaywiwin musical instrument—water drum, birch bark rattle and drum beater.

9

prehistoric ways had been abandoned, as an example, rather than furs being hung in the lodge various types of cloth were hung.

Warren wrote, "I was once standing near the entrance of an Ojibway Medewigan, more commonly known as the Grand Medicine Lodge while the inmates were busy in the performance of the varied ceremonies of this, their chief medical and religious rite. The lodge measured in length about 100 feet, and fifteen in width, was built partially covered along the sides with green boughs of the balsam tree. On a pole raised horizontally above its whole length were hung pieces of cloth, calico, handkerchiefs, blankets, etc.,—the offerings or the sacrifices of the novice who was about to be initiated into the mysteries of the Midaywiwin Society. The lodge was full of men and women who sat in a row along both sides. None but those who had been initiated were allowed to enter. They were dressed and painted in their best and most fancy clothing and colors, and each held in his hand the midawiaun or medicine sack, which consisted of bird skins, stuffed otter, beaver and snake skins.

This account tells how the novice to be initiated sat in the center on a clean mat facing the Medawautig which is a cedar post planted in the center of the lodge, painted red and decorated with tufts of bird down.

Warren continues, "The four grave looking We-kauns, or initiating priests stood around him with their medicine sacks, drums and rattles. One of the four We-kauns, after addressing a few remarks to the novice in a low voice, took from his medicine sack, the Medamegis, a small white sea-shell, which is the chief emblem of the Miday rite. Holding this on the palm of his hand, he ran slowly around the inside of the lodge, displaying it to the inmates, and followed by his fellow We-kauns swinging their rattles and exclaiming in a deep guttural tone, "Whe, whe, when. Circling the lodge in this impressive manner, on coming again to the novice, they stopped running, uttering a deep sonorous, "What-ho-ho-ho." They then quietly walked off, and taking their stand at the western end of the lodge, the leader still displaying the shell on the palm of his hand, delivered a loud and spirited harangue.

The language and the phrases used were so obscure to a common listener, that it would be impossible to give a literal translation of the whole speech. The following passage, however, forcibly struck my

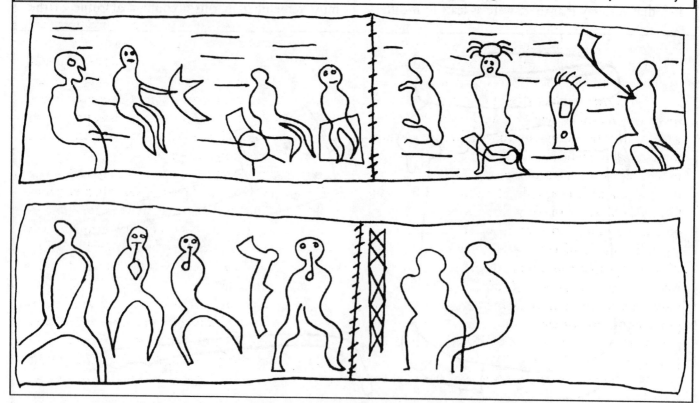

Four sections of Midaywiwin scrolls—these are sewn together in pairs. Because of their abstraction, they cannot be interpreted.

attention:

"While our forefathers were living on the great salt water toward the rising sun, the great Megis (sea shell) showed itself above the surface of the great water, and the rays of the sun for a long period were reflected from its glossy back. It gave warmth and light to the An-ish-in-aub-ag (red race). All at once it sank into the deep and for a time it gave life to our forefathers, and reflected back the rays of the sun. Again it disappeared from sight and it rose not, till it appeared to the eyes of the An-ish-in-aub-ag on the shores of the first great lake. Again it sank from sight, and death daily visited the wigwams of our forefathers, till it showed its back, and reflected the rays of the sun once more at Bow-e-ting (Sault St. Marie, Michigan). Here it remained for a long time, but once more, and for the last time, it disappeared, and the Anish-in-aub-ag was left in darkness and misery, till it floated and once more showed its bright back at Mo-ning-wn-a-kaungin (La Pointe Island), where it has ever since reflected back the rays of the sun, and blessed our ancestors with life, light and wisdom. Its rays reach the remotest village of the wide spread Ojibways."

During his entire discourse the old We-kaun continued to display the sacred shell—the object of their faith. Warren desired to obtain an explanation as to what the speech meant exactly, and so presenting the We-kaun with a gift of tobacco and cloth for leggings persuaded him to reveal the meaning.

The priest explained to him what the megis spoken of meant in Miday religion. He continued with a curious statement that in the beginning sounds as though he may have incorporated reincarnation into his system of beliefs, "Our forefathers, many string of lives ago, lived on the shores of the Great Salt Water in the east. There seems to be some obscure meaning in the "string of lives" statement.

The we-kaun continued, "Here it was that while congregated in a great town, and while they were suffering the ravages of sickness and death, the Great Spirit, the intercession of Manabozho, the great common uncle of the An-ish-in-aub-ag, granted them this rite wherewith life is restored and prolonged.

Our fore fathers moved from the shores of the great water and proceeded westward. The Medaywiwin lodge was pulled down and it was not again erected, till our forefathers again took a stand on the shores of the great river near where Mo-ne-sung (Montreal) now stands.

"In the course of time this town was again deserted, and our forefathers still proceeded westward, lit not their fires till they reached the shores of Lake Huron, where again the rites of the Midaywiwin were practiced.

Lake Huron, by the way, is less than a ½ mile from Old Van Etten Creek where I found the Miday stone pendant. Thunder Bay where the discs of chapter two were found is part of Lake Huron.

The priest continued to explain to Warren, "Again these rites were forgotten, and the Midaywiwin lodge was not built till the Ojibways found themselves congregated at Bow-e-ting (outlet of Lake Superior), where it remained for many winters. Still the Ojibway moved westward, and for the last time the Midaywiwin lodge was erected on the island of La Pointe, and here, long before the pale face appeared among them, it was practiced in its purest and most original form. Many of our fathers lived the full term of life granted to mankind by the Great Spirit, and the forms of many old people were mingled with each rising generation. This my grandson is the meaning of the words you did not understand; they have been repeated to us by our forefathers for many generations."

For every ceremony a goskidibagan or medicine skin is given to the participants. Twelve different skins were used in the following order; otter, mink, owl, snake, bear paw, grizzly claw, portion of bear hide, the skin and feathers from the breast of a turkey, gray squirrel, and weasel.

Those in attendance at a Midaywiwin rite carry the medicine skin he was given when he sponsored a ceremony. Being that there is no limit to how many times a member might go through such ceremonies he may have had a favorite skin which he carried, or often times it was the one used in the preceding ceremony.

Early accounts tell that the skin and megis were buried with individual members when they died and archaeological excavations prove this. In historic times, though, items meant to represent the skin and megis are all that is buried. The reason being the powerful forces behind the megis may indeed cause the corpse to re-animate and leave the grave behind!

Imagine if you will that this is true. Zombie like creatures spawned by the Great Lakes area Midaywiwin Society? It has been claimed that disinterments prove this as fact—at least among the Indians. If such is the case perhaps some of the ancients still walk the mystical shores of Michigan's Great Lakes!

An interesting side note at this point concerns the Chippewa belief that the first earth and its red inhabitants somehow made the Great Spirit/Gitchi Manitou so mad that he unleashed a flood on the face of the earth to destroy his creation. Sounds a little bit familiar doesn't it?

Manabozho who we discussed earlier acted as an intermediate and saved the red race allowing them to dwell safely on the earth. In fact Manabozho taught them how to farm, hunt and to cure the sick. He also gave them tobacco which was of great significance socially and religiously to the American Indian nation wide.

Manabozho was not without his faults though, he was also a trickster and his antics are found throughout woodland tradition.

Modern day Midaywiwin rites have become homogenized, weakened by the influence of white missionary work. It is rumored that the pure rites are performed in secret, and that the mixed up rites are performed for benefit of the curious. Though written accounts indicate that there is also strong power in today's Midaywiwin and in the megis.

W. Vernon Kinietz in his book *The Chippewa Village,* describes a modern day (about 1946) Miday healing rite. Mr. Kinietz lived among the Chippewa at Lac Vieux Desert. He reported, "As now constituted the Midaywiwin is a ceremony given by an individual either to gain health or to insure its continuance. A sick person or his family is seldom able to arrange a ceremony during the illness but he is given the benefits according to the following ritual. when a person is sick and the other remedies fail the shaman usually prescribes a session of the Midaywiwin. If the patient or the family agrees to put on the rite the shaman fastens a megis around the patients neck, either threaded on raw hide string or sewed in a flap of such a string. The power, health giving and otherwise, of the ceremony is symbolized by the megis. The act of fastening on the megis is

called borrowing life. Wearing a megis is a sign that one is living on borrowed time as it were and sooner or later must clear up the account by putting on the Midaywiwin (ceremony). This is supposed to be within a year but sometimes goes two years or more.

Conducting the "owed" ceremony takes much preparation. Feasts have to be given and some alcoholic drink must be on hand. There have to be gifts and those who erect the poles for the lodge have to be paid.

The day prior to the ceremony the Midewigan is made ready. Its frame work is bare and unattended until a ceremony is called. Preparations consist of repairing the frame. The frame is made up of saplings which are pounded into the ground in two rows twelve feet apart, these are then bent together in pairs. These poles form an arch about seven feet tall. In appearance it is not unlike long houses inhabited by Indians in prehistoric times. The entire building is much like an elongated dome.

The ends of the lodge are made in fashion by poles again being pounded into the ground in a half circle and are then bent in and tied to the arches. The completed lodge is about 70 feet in length.

Kinietz told of covering the frame work by standing pieces of cedar bark against the outside of the framework. He explains that, "starting with the east doorway these slabs which are about five feet long and from one or two feet in width are put in place with each slightly over lapping the previous one and fastened with saplings placed horizontally across the slabs and lashed to the inner framework. The cedar bark covers only the sides of the lodge. The top of the lodge is covered with birch bark. The bark is cut three feet wide and sewn together to form rolls fifteen to twenty feet long. One roll is laid lengthwise along each side of the lodge overlapping the top of the cedar bark slabs. The spaces between the two sheets of birch bark are covered with a third.

The entire ceremony, as far as is known, is quite lengthy. An Ouskabawis or courier distributes the invitations to the Miday ceremony. He begins with a dish of tobacco and small sticks in the amount of the number of persons to be invited. If the person contacted is going to attend he signifies by taking a stick and also partaking of the tobacco.

As all ready stated, music is a large part of the Miday ceremony and because of this great care was taken in the preparation of the instruments used. The drum, as in most Indian religions, plays a highly significant part in the ceremony.

The drum used in the Miday rites is 16 inches tall and eight inches in diameter. It is made of basswood or cedar. The drum is thicker at the bottom than at the top, and has a wooden bottom. About ½ way down the side a small hole is made in which water can be poured, the hole is plugged up with a small wooden peg. The drum head is kept moist. There is virtually no decoration except for a red circle in the center of the wooden bottom.

The drum stick is special also. One end of the stick is carved in the effigy form of a birds head. The stick is about 18 inches in length.

A rattle is also used. In ancient times it was made from turtle shell, birch bark or even a gourd. Birch bark, being sacred to the Chippewa, was probably the most widely used medium.

W. Vernon Kinietz is one of the few whites to actually witness the sacred ceremonies, back in the 1940's. His descriptions are vivid and I would like to quote a little from them about the ceremony itself.

"Instructions in each degree of the Midaywiwin is given the candidates orally and by means of drawings in sand. Besides the drawings, which do not amount to much, there are little wooden figures to represent the different gods, the Miday and the candidate. The principal instruction is by means of these figures. The actions of the dancers, the location of the presents, the seats of the gods, and the positions of the candidate himself at different stages of the ceremony are shown by means of these figures."

I will interrupt the narrative here only to ask a question I can not answer. What gods? Are their secret gods of the Chippewa that whites do not know about? We know that there are three principal gods, but Kinietz indicates in the following narrative that there may be as many as 12 gods present during the Miday ceremony. In trying to secure an answer to this for this book I found that no Indian would discuss details of the Midaywiwin with me, but this is what I expected.

Kinietz continues, "At the conclusion of the ceremony the sticks representing the gods are given to the candidate along with a pinch of sand used and some of the tobacco passed at the dance. The sticks are kept by the candidates for a year and then placed at the foot of a tree or some other place with some tobacco to ask favors or continuation of health. As far as I could find out, there was no special sand used, just wet sand. It was pressed into a rectangle approximately four inches by twelve inches and about two inches in height. The wooden figures were about an inch and a half to two inches in length and shaped like a carrot with a little ball on the large end.

"There are 12 gods present at each meeting of the Midaywiwin. The one outside of each door is its guardian. The one outside the east door has to be placated before entering the lodge. In the song sung before entering, the phrase—'I am mentioned,' occurs frequently. This is to tell the guardian of the door that the singer has been mentioned in the Modewigan and so it is all right for him to enter.

"I was able to observe nothing in the ceremony that included the participation of the four gods represented by the sides of the door. All six of the interior spots were included during the ceremony. In each round of the lodge, either by the Miday and his assistant alone, or when they headed a procession of dancers, each of these six spots had a rattle shaken once very vigorously at it and the drum also dipped towards it at the same time that it was given a sharp stroke."

Of the Midaywiwin we can find the tangible remains of its existence through archaeological means as I employed.

There are also the myths handed down from many generations of Indians which speak of its origin. There are even a few accounts of white people who were allowed to observe the ceremonies. However, there is one thing you will not find and that is any insight into the actual healing rituals performed by the Miday priest. These remain secret and probably all ways will.

I called the Chippewa tribal center at Sault St. Marie, Michigan and asked for information about the secret ceremonies. The only response I could get is, "We can not talk about such things, they are sacred to us alone. But the original rituals are concealed even from those descended of the great old ones who performed them in the now dim past of the Great Lakes area."

Chapter Two:
Mystery Religions
of Northeast
Michigan Woodlands

For those of you who have never visited northeast Michigan let me tell you a little about it. The coastline forms the west shore of Lake Huron, one of the Great Lakes. Lake Huron figures prominently in the religious beliefs and customs of this section. Huron's beaches are for the most part sandy, and during the summer provide some of the most delightful tanning spots to be found.

Oddly though, as you move north from the

small city of Harrisville, 10 miles along the lake shore to the "ghost town" of Black River, then still further north about four more miles, you find that the beach and atmosphere make a dramatic shift.

At this point you are miles from anywhere, water on one side and dense pine forest on the other. Suddenly the sandy beach gives way to rocks and pebbles creating a very harsh look. The air here takes on a chill even during the hot summer. It is here that thousands of years ago the great glaciers which carved out this hilly area stopped and deposited the rubble which is strewn on the lake shore. But this stretch of beach lasts only about four miles.

Further north about a mile and a half the pine forest suddenly gives way to an abrupt clearing where no trees grow and the wild grass never attains a height of more than two or three feet. Here you are at the precipice of a great unsolved mystery; but only one of many possibly interconnected mysteries that dot this ancient area.

This area is known locally as South Point, named for a small finger like peninsula of land which juts out into the lake. The rocky beach here begins to once more give way to the sand. However, just under the surface of the sand are large rocks. As you walk from the small peninsula into the clearing these large stones look as though they were placed purposely to form a large walk way.

In years past, Jerry Wagner, a local historian excavated from this site a large thunder bird effigy made from a green stone boulder. The thunder bird was revered by the natives who lived here. As you walk in from the lake the shore takes an abrupt rise. In the shore line there is a large depression, a dug out area now long grown over with grass. It is enough for now to know that this "chamber" of sorts is here—we will discuss it later on.

Walking through the clearing you can not help asking yourself why the pine forest is so close but has not filled this clearing in. Mr. Wagner speculated in times past perhaps something unnatural occurred and contaminated the land.

At the edge of the clearing the trees begin once more a profuse growth. At the edge of the clearing is found what is known locally as a stone well. It is a hole about five feet deep lined with stones in a dry construction manner, that is to say no mortar was used.

In a short distance among the trees is the "great mystery," this is known as the Black River Stone Works. This is a series of so called stone fences which form a rectangular shape and cover about 2 acres of ground. Periodically in the walls are breaks, or gate like openings. The stones are loosely, but neatly piled and in height are about three to four feet. Surrounding the walls are conical piles of stones about four and a half feet tall. From our cultural perspective no practical use for these stone works can be arrived at.

Such stone fences and piles are found through out the United States, and are particularly significant in terms of burial practices and thus passage into the next plane of existence. In Michigan they can possibly be tied to the bizarre "Feast of the Dead" which will be described shortly.

Salvatore Michael Trento in his book *The Search For Lost America* (Contemporary Books/ 1978) says of these mysterious stone piles, "Stone heaps come in many shapes and sizes. Some are as large as 60 feet in diameter and 8 feet in height, while others are little more than 2 feet by 2 feet. Endless speculation has arisen over the origin and function of the cairns (piles). James Adair, whose History of the American Indian appeared in 1775, felt that the Indians raised those heaps merely to do honor to their dead, and incite the living to the pursuit of virtue. Earlier books all mentioned passing Indians throwing rocks onto existing piles. And even Washington Irving, high above the Hudson River at his dreamy Sunnyside Estate, told a similar story in a fanciful essay entitled, "Traits of the Indian Character."

Elton Davis, a popular historian/archaeologist told me of his thoughts pertaining to the mysterious

Sioux tepee by Fiske Fort July -17-

15

stone works at Black River.

"My wife Kathy and I first hiked up there during the summer of 1986. It was fascinating to say the least and we made many additional trips as time went on. We took numerous stereo photographs which identify both the stone piles as well as the stone walls."

Davis continued, "Each of the stone piles is hollowed out. In a number of the piles large trees have grown up attesting to their age. Having done much work over the years at South Point I can say that there is a co-mingling of cultures at this site. That is to say I have personally seen many artifacts from this site that are only as old as the 1850's. But there are also relics of great antiquity; Celts, arrow heads which leaves no doubt as to the Indian influence here. There is a large boulder on a path not far from the stone works whose surface is pecked away at, it was no doubt used a ceremonial mortar.

"Another interesting feature of the stone walls. They ramble, run straight for hundreds of feet, then for no apparent rhyme or reason, unexpectedly veer off at acute right angles. Within their confines however, exist many, many stone piles. Some are 12 feet or more across and about 5 feet in height. It is possible for a man to climb down into the center of these conical piles and remain standing."

Great pains were employed to make certain these stone piles endured the ages. Very specific stones were selected and carefully fitted into place. But care was always of the utmost concern when preparing these sites which may have been portals for the soul to cross over to the next world.

No excavations have yet been conducted at this site, nor are any planned, which might confirm their exact purpose. Nonetheless, we may speculate upon their purpose from other stone piles which have been excavated.

As an example I will again turn to Mr. Trento's book, *The Ssearch For Lost America.*

Trento states, "In the late 1880's the Smithsonian excavated a mound on a farm near Patterson, North Carolina, and discovered some surprising remains. Agents for the Institution showed that several skeletons and stone piles had been simultaneously buried beneath the earthen mound. The piles accompanying the skeletons seemed to confirm age old legends about the sites being repositories for the dead."

The Black River site compares favorably with a site located at Ramapo, New York. There is found a tremendous construction of stone walls covering nearly 200 acres! This network of walls also consists of many stone piles. Like the Black River site this New York site is located in a heavily wooded area near a fresh water source. Purely speculative of course but might not the Indian mind, so used to traveling the water ways with his birch bark and dug out canoes, have visualized the spirits of his dead comrades as using these water ways to pass to the land of the souls thus their close placement to the waters?

About 200 feet from the stone works is a depression in the high lake shore. Local archaeologist Jerry Wagner years ago conducted excavations into this unusual feature and found that it had at one time been used around the 1850's. I suggest though that it may have been used then but that its original use was much earlier and in connection with the stone fences and piles. Mr. Wagner found pieces of old china as well as antique spoons and forks, he also went through reddish sand where timbers had long ago rotted to their base elements. Such

chambers are not unusual in connection with fences and piles in other areas of the country.

In New England many of these chambers still exist as they were made from stone slabs, but at Black River no slab stones could be found and so the next best material was employed—wood. In particular, four miles from a stone work in Thompson, Connecticut a group of five slab roofed chambers were located. Like the Black River chamber these are relatively small, 10 feet in diameter and 4 feet in height, almost the exact dimensions of the Black River chamber.

An unusual feature indeed, but gut instinct speaks to me that this was the point of departure for the souls to take sail across Lake Huron. This chamber is, by the way, at the edge of the mysterious clearing spoken of earlier.

There is another interesting similarity between the Black River Stone Works and those found in New York. The New York stone works are located near a large 10 by 7 foot cut stone block that was conceived by the Shohola Indians as being the "eye of the universe." You must picture this site to feel the spiritual forces that radiate from it. It is located on the Shohola Creek in an opening in the forest, a restful setting which would induce meditation on one's self and nature. The local Indians it is said

came from miles around to meditate on this stone as to them it was the center of creation.

The Black River Stone Works is not far from the center of Indian religious beliefs throughout the northeast woodlands, that being Mackinaw Island.

All powerful of the spirits to these Indians was the turtle spirit, and Mackinaw was thought to be the great turtle. Indeed as you observe it from the main land it looks much like a tremendous turtle swimming in the Straits of Mackinaw. Mackinaw Island was considered the earthly abode or dwelling place of Gitchi Manitou/The Great Spirit—the supreme god. The waters that caress the shell of the mystical Great Turtle are those of none other than Lake Huron!

Mackinaw is bathed in legends of the northern woodland Indians. It is to them the "eye of the universe" just as is the great cut stone slab of New York. By the way, that slab is in itself an enigma as with the tools the Indians of that region had they could not have possibly cut such a stone block; then who did?

We will return to Black River in a bit, but while we are at Mackinaw Island lets just skip about five miles over the water to the town of St. Ignace. Here a mass grave was discovered and excavated some time ago. This mass grave was the repository

17

for bones gathered together for the "Feast of the Dead." In fact bones from as far away as Black River may have ended up in this mass grave. The souls sailed out from South Point across Lake Huron to the next world, but the bones may have traveled north up Lake Huron to St. Ignace. Lets take a look at this unusual feast.

The festival of the dead was held about every 12 years or as ordered by the councils of neighboring villages. At this time, the remains of those who have died and been buried individually are dug up and brought together for a feast with the living— and what a feast.

The job of carrying the bones of the relatives from the cemetery fell to the women, and if the flesh had not been all consumed then it was up to the ladies to cleanse the bones. The bones were wrapped up in fine new beaver skins and adorned with beads and necklaces that were provided by friends and family.

W. Vernon Kinietz in his informative book, *Indians of the Western Great Lakes 1615–1760* reported, "The contributors would say: Behold, here is what I give for the bones of my father, my mother, my uncle, my cousin, or other relatives. And putting them in a new sack they carry them on their backs; they also decorate the top of the sack with a number of little ornaments, necklaces, bracelets, and other embellishments. Then the pelt, hatchets, kettles and other things that they reckon of value, with a quantity of provisions, are also carried to their destination, and when all are assembled there they put their food in one place to be used in feast, which are a great expense to them, and then hang up decently in the cabins of their hosts all their sacks and pelts, while awaiting the day on which all must be buried in the ground.

"Outside the village a large and deep pit is dug which will accommodate the bones and grave offerings. On the precipice of the pit was built a large platform. Very special care was taken in the preparation of the pit. It was lined on the bottom and side with beaver skins and robes. Then the grave goods were placed in using a layered fashion. For example; axes then kettles, beads, necklaces, bracelets and so on. This completed the chief, from the platform, dumped out all the bones from the sacks into the pit among the merchandise. All this is then covered with dirt and wooden poles were pounded into the ground around the pit. A covering was affixed to the poles. The covering was made sturdy, made to last as long as possible."

A missionary, Brebeuf in 1636 wrote about the feast in such a way as to truly bring it to life. Of the conclusion of the feast he did particular justice when he related, "As we drew near, we saw nothing less than a picture of hell. The large space (pit) was quite full of fires and flames, and the air resounded in all directions with the confused voices of these Indians; their noise ceased, however, for some time, and they began to sing, but in voices so sorrowful and lugubrious that it represented to us the horrible sadness and the abyss of despair into which these unhappy souls are forever plunged." To call these souls unhappy called for a judgment of the author,

Chief Gall, a Hunkpapa Dakota who, early in his acquaintance with the photographer, threatened him with a weapon. They later became friends, and David F. Barry photographed him many times.

in fact I would assume that the participants being buried were viewed as quite happy.

His account continues, "Nearly all the souls were thrown in when we arrived, for it was done almost in the turning of a hand; each one had made haste, thinking there would not be enough room for all the souls; we saw, however, enough of it to judge of the rest. There were five or six in the pit, arranging the bones with poles. The pit was full within about two feet; they turned back over the bones and the robes which bordered the edge of the pit, and covered the remaining space with mats and bark. Then they heaped the pit with sand, poles and wooden stakes, which they threw in without order. Some women brought to it some dishes of corn; and that day, and the following days, several cabins of the village provided nets quite full of corn which were thrown upon the pit." But I have digressed far to much, lets make our way back down Lake Huron's shores to South Point and the mystery there. The stone fences, pits and the unusual chamber are all part of the religious expression of the Indians dwelling in the pine forests of the northeast woodlands.

From South Point, Thunder Bay begins. Thunder Bay is unusual and you need camp at South Point but once to discover how the bay got its name. There is at certain times the unmistakable sound of thunder produced by some phenomenon unknown to me. Kathy and I both were amazed by this on numerous trips to the stone works.

At Thunder Bay near the city of Alpena, Michigan and on the site of the Alpena Community College, was made another unique find also of religious significance to the natives of the area. What was found are the Naub-cow-zo-win discs.

Picture if you will a harsh, wind swept bay.

This body of water abounds with dangers which were inflicted upon the native travelers by the spirits unless they were appeased by offerings of some sort. Visualize also an Indian shaman attempting to devise a way to insure safety for his people who were forced to cross these waters or even dwell on their shores.

Over 200 discs made of shale have been found at four sites clustered around the mouth of Thunder Bay. They were manufactured here. Many of the discs are blank, however, many bear inscribed images of spiritual entities who were very powerful to the Indians of the northeast. In fact many of the images can also be found on the birch bark scrolls of the Midaywiwin as described in chapter one.

Prominently displayed is the evil form of "Me-she-pe-shiw," who was found on no less than 16 discs! Me-she-pe-shiw is a wicked mountain lion who is believed to live beneath the waters of the Great Lakes. The creature is said to cause violent storms by the movement of its great tail. Perhaps these "amulets" were devised to do honor to the wicked one and thus appease him. Sacrifices were also made to Me-she-pe-shiw of tobacco and sacred dogs.

Other disc amulets recovered may have been made to evoke the protective power of the entities inscribed on them. Ne-gig, the Great Otter who figures very highly in the creation myth is also among the roster of spiritual figures depicted.

The Great Otter, as discussed in chapter one, is the basic symbolism for the righteous in the Midaywiwin Society. Otter skin was a preferred material for use in the medicine bags used in the Midaywiwin ceremonies.

Ah-ne-mi-ke, the great Thunder Bird is also represented. His power was vast and the creature was both feared and revered. According to tradition the Thunder Birds live above the western sky. They have control over thunder and lightening both powerful nature forces. Allegedly the lightening bolts which the Thunder Birds are able to throw are used to deter the actions of the evil spirits such as Me-she-pe-shiw.

Less important on the discs would appear to be, Moz the moose. This images appears on a single disc. Amik the beaver also appears on a disc. Perhaps most importantly is the depiction of trees on the discs. I would like to quote a passage from *Naub-cow-zo-win Discis From Northern Michigan* by Charles E. Cleland, Richard D. Clute and Robert Haltiner (Midcontinental Journal of Archaeology/1984). They reported that, "The most frequent and most enigmatic of the symbols on the discs of the Haltiner collection shows what appears to represent a tree rising from the mountain. This symbol represents the Great Medicine Tree, Michi-gi-zhik which in Algonquian mythology is identified with the northern white cedar and is a source of herbal knowledge. Michi-gi-zhik grows at the center of the earth and symbolically interconnects the four vertical layers of the Algonquin cosmos, that is, the underworld, earth, air, and the sky above."

Also found on the discs is a star symbol not unlike the star burst design of the pendant in chapter one. The meaning of this symbol is obscured by the mists of time.

That stones should be used in the manufacture of amulets is not surprising as stones themselves were believed by the Indians to have great power. The power of stones and their great significance will be detailed in a later chapter.

Between Alpena and South Point is the small community of Ossineke, and running near Ossineke is the Devil River. Here is another of those very mysterious places where the spirits seem to congregate. Shin-ga-baw, the Divine Chief put down many image stones along the banks of the Devil River—in fact Ossineke means image stone.

The chief told his people that when he died his spirit would come back to the place of the Image Stones at the mouth of the Devil River. At the mouth of the Devil River, which was named because of the big marshes there that were very difficult to cross, there stood in 1839 two ancient stones worshiped as sacred by the Indians of the area. One was composed of gneiss with varying bands of quartz, and it is said that it had the appearance of being worked into its shape by the action of the water. Its estimated weight was 300 pounds. The second stone was about four feet long and resembled the shape of a man's body minus head, arms and legs. One very old document describes it as, "Having the appearance of having been molded from lake sand, the surface being concreted with some substance resembling bark. It was hard on the outside, but soft and crumbly on the inside.

These stones had mysterious powers as was attested to by a report penned by David O. Oliver an historian of Thunder River country back in the 1870's.

According to his report the origin of these sacred stones about which hovered the spirit of the Divine Chief Shin-ga-baw, is lost in antiquity, "but it is handed down in legend that hostile tribesmen raided the sacred grounds of the Chippewas, captured two of the latter, and, taking their captives and the sacred stones in a canoe, started across Thunder Bay. Reaching the middle of the bay, they threw overboard the stones. The water immediately boiled up and drowned the raiders, while the captive Chippewas safely returned to shore in the canoe, only to find the stones in their former place. The sacred stones are no longer on the banks of the river."

It seemed that when the people they served were gone so also was their power. It is said that during the mid 1800's a fisherman who put ashore at the mouth of the river needed anchors for his fishing nets and took the stones for that purpose. This time they did not make a supernatural return as before, but now presumably rest somewhere on the bottom of Lake Huron.

Although it has little bearing on the religious beliefs of the Indians who inhabited this mystical area it is interesting to note that both sides of the Devil River were occupied by Indian burying grounds. In a burial mound by the river was found a trepanned human skull showing that these ancients of the Huron shore who are considered by science as not having achieved a very high degree of civilization were capable of brain surgery!

Also adding to the mystic and charm of the spirit inhabited area is the fact that the limestone soil is heavily impregnated with meteorites, reportedly weighing from a half pound to a half ton. These dropped at some unknown time in the past when as legend has it the tail of a meteorite sideswiped the earth.

The Lake Huron shores are indeed an mystical place where the spirits of the past dwell and perhaps still influence the lives of those yet living upon these shores. Certainly not all the stones of the Lake Huron region have lost their power as you will learn shortly.

Chapter Three: The Sacred Image Stone and Powers of the Rocks

August of 1986 was particularly hot across the northeast United States. On the day in question my dog, Samson, in an effort to keep cool had dug a hole by his house. Kathy and I always have our eyes open for relics of ancient man. While taking Samson a pan of cold water, Kathy discovered in the dirt that he had kicked up, three prehistoric Indian pot shards.

She was quite excited about this for several reasons. First, after hunting for and finding relics of ancient man all across north east Michigan, we had never considered looking in our own back yard. Second, the find was made directly next to a small building in which we had established a museum to display our treasured finds. The odds of finding such material next to this building by the dog who had been put there to protect our finds must be very high indeed.

Kathy and I got our equipment together and began digging with eager anticipation at what might be below the surface of the ground that we had been daily walking over. In fact I was so excited that I called into work sick so that I could carry out these excavations.

By the time we had completed our work late that same afternoon, we had excavated a four by five foot area. We had also unearthed some 1,500 pot shards (pieces of broken pottery vessels) which represented two pottery vessels.

The way the pots were arranged in the ground it looked as though they had just been left standing there and finally fell in on themselves from climactic aging. I packed these pieces away with the intent of trying to reassemble them during the winter months.

There was quite a lot of other material collected. The ground yielded to us a Hopewell style arrowhead, an unfinished ground green stone, a portion of a human arm bone, a human head in profile fetish, hundreds of pieces of flint, and the subject of this chapter—a stone which resembled a Celt, which is to say, an ungrooved stone ax.

This stone did not really have the appearance of having been worked by the hand of ancient man. I felt it had its peculiar shape quite by the design of nature. None-the-less, by its positioning among the

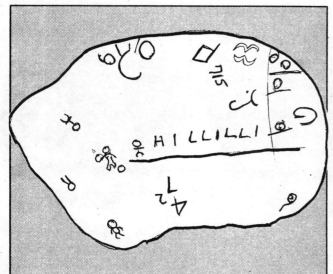

Sketch of the various "figures" and "symbols" that have appeared on the rock starting in November, 1986.

other relics there can be no doubt that it served some purpose for the prehistoric people who had lived in my backyard. For me, the stone held a certain fascination which I could not explain. I took the stone and set it down on a nearby bench to examine more closely when our work was finished. I am ashamed to admit that I forgot all about the stone for a while—almost three months to be exact!

Early in November as the weather was becoming cold and inclement I dug out (with no pun intended) the pottery shards and worked day and night trying to fit together as many of them as I could. Of the 1,500 pieces I was able to assemble 17 of the larger ones. These formed a section of pot 12 x 7 inches in size.

I was very pleased to have been able to assemble anything from this 3 dimensional jig saw puzzle that had no picture to go by. I decided to take my work over to Jerry Wagner, an avocational archeologist like myself, to get his opinion. As I was packing the pottery I suddenly remembered the Celt like stone I had left in the backyard in the summer. In reflection it seems odd that I should remember the stone at that particular moment out of the clear blue. I retrieved the stone from the bench in the backyard where it had sat since I took it from the ground. I examined it carefully, then packed it with the pottery as I wanted to get Jerry's input on this piece also.

When I arrived at Jerry's home on the evening of November 25th, he was anxious to see the pottery. Jerry informed me that he had never seen such a large reconstruction from our area. I had wanted to show him the Celt like stone first, sort of save the best for last, but he took the pottery from the bag I had packed it in.

As Jerry's wife Marilyn watched on he set up the pottery on the floor of his living room, propping it up with the Celt like stone. Jerry began making all sorts of measurements, and for the next 45 minutes we had a very in depth discussion about the pot and the people who had built the pot perhaps as much as 2,000 years ago. In point of fact, I was so engrossed by the conversation that it seemed almost as though we were surrounded by those ancient people.

After we had exhausted our conversation Jerry

Center disc portrays the all-powerful Thunderbird. Photo by Robert E. Haltiner

picked up the pottery and gently handed it to me. I placed it back in the bag as he lifted the Celt and said to me, "Dennis, what are these markings?"

I thought at first that he was joking as there had not been a trace of anything on the stone when I examined it before packing it. Now however, there was a string of letter like symbols across the face of the stone. What was really uncanny is that they felt slightly raised from the stone. All three of us were shocked to say the least.

We have never been able to come up with a plausible explanation for the symbols. We wondered if somehow contact between the stone and the pottery had made them appear. Perhaps our in depth discussion had somehow contributed.

Upon returning home with this stone my first thought was to try and photograph the symbols. The camera lens kept fogging up and the pictures came back over exposed. This in itself was a mystery to me as I am a pretty good photographer. All was not lost though as the symbols could still be seen though it was faintly. These symbols began to fade

after I did the photographs. By the following morning they were completely gone. There was however much more to come.

As I said the photographs came back over exposed. I took them to a photo studio and had them enhanced by computer. On the photographs were symbols that we had missed before due to their small size in comparison to the main "letters. There were stick figures. One of the figures resembled a man holding a bow, still another looked like a man running down a path. These smaller figures were very similar in appearance to rock art found throughout the northeast and to a lesser extent on the Midaywiwin Society scrolls.

There was no reason to expect that there would be anything else unusual happening with the stone, but much more did. The "image stones" most active day was on November 28th, 1986. Jerry and I had been invited to a special after Thanksgiving Day dinner at the home of a friend and publisher in Commins, Michigan. Neither of our wives were able to attend. Being at least a forty five minute drive we

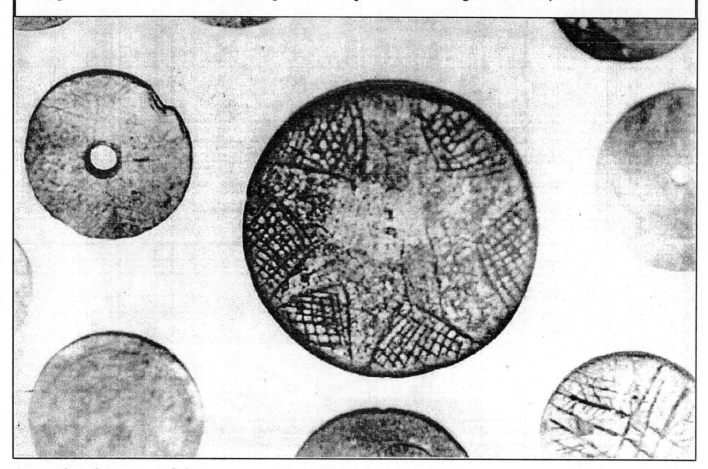

Center disc shows one of the many ways the "star burst" is used in northeast woodland context. Photo by Robert E. Haltiner

took the stone with us and examined it very closely. There was not the slightest sign of any symbols across the face of the stone.

The stone had become a favorite topic of conversation between Jerry and I. There were eight people at dinner that night. I guided the conversation so that we could discuss the stone. Jerry described to the eagerly listening audience what had happened on the evening of the 25th. After hearing about the stone all were in agreement that they wanted to see it. I excused myself from the table and went to the car to retrieve the stone.

When I reached the car I could tell right away that the image stone was beginning to do something again. A dark circle was forming on the face of the stone. The dark area looked sticky but did not feel that way to the touch. It resembled a substance that was wet and appeared that it was actually being secreted from the stone.

Unlike in the first instance, this time the image was not raised from the stone. When I took it in and showed everyone they were all amazed and excited. A man who I had not seen before nor since held the

stone and over the next hour much happened.

Many symbols appeared on the face of the mystic stone in rapid succession. Indeed the images were appearing so fast that we were unable to copy them all down. A symbol looking like an open topped four appeared along with the numbers 2 and 7, then the open four changed to an old fashioned pointed four. The action of the changes reminded me of how numbers change on the face of a digital watch. The original dark circle changed from just a circle to a circle with lines extending out of it. This gave the stone an eerie resemblance to a face in profile, the circle being the eye with lashes. I wondered at the time if this might not represent seeing something—something from the past? Two other small circles appeared, one with a sort of tail. These were on either side of the larger circle.

At some point during the on going events, Mike, the man who was holding the stone handed it over to the lady sitting next to him and hurriedly left. He was rather unnerved by what was occurring.

The circle was still there when Jerry and I left for home about 7:00 PM. On the way home we

This disc represents the evil Me-she-pe-shiw. Photo by Robert E. Haltiner.

24

pulled off the road and turned on the car light. We examined the stone to see if any further changes had taken place. The eye like circle was still there. In the excitement I had completely forgotten that my camera was in the car. Here on the side of M72 I snapped several pictures and then we returned to our respective homes.

There was one more occurrence that evening and this time it was observed by my wife Kathy, and my mother, Lorrain. The circle was still present with the alleged eyebrows. Over this formed a symbol which looked a stylized number eight. This also faded fast and a photo produced no image. The stone seemed to have spent most of its energy by this point and was running out of steam.

Its activity became sporadic and nothing more appeared until the 30th of November. Symbols that resembled the numbers 7, 1, and 5 appeared and a short time later a diamond shape with a sort of tail. On December 5th towards one end of the image stone there appeared light veins of gold and one of silver. These lasted for several days. Other vague shadowy figures appeared on the stone through the first of January 1987. Few of these later symbols were well enough defined to make out, and they were fast in appearing and just as quick in fading.

In the summer of 1987 my brother in law, Marlin Marx Jr., and I, dowsed the area where the

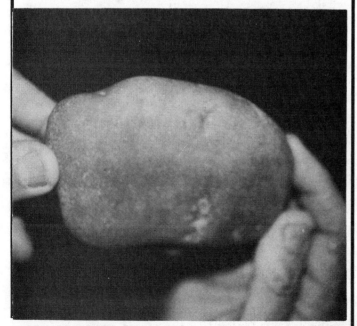

Author holds mysterious "talisman" discovered in his backyard, the surface of which is said to "change," sometimes rapidly, sometimes over a period of time.

relics had been found. We used two coat hangers bent in "L" shape. Until this day I was a confirmed skeptic when it came to dowsing. As we walked across my backyard the rods would cross at the exact perimeter of where our digging began, remain crossed while walking across the area we had dug and then uncross at the other side. A dozen or so tries produced the same results even with me doing the dowsing!

There was nothing left there in the way of relics so the reaction of the rods seemed very unusual to me. There is of course the possibility that there could be a deep burial there. But if there were no other relics there was some residual power left in this ground where the image stone had lain for centuries which was detected by the rods. Because I had the property up for sale and was in the process of moving to Greenbush, Michigan no further excavations were carried out.

I have always felt that further excavations might have held the key to the symbols, as when using the dowsing rods, Marlin and I found several other areas that produced the same effect. The area we were able to excavate was really quite small.

In looking at the relics that were found with the image stone there are several unique things. First of all is why was there only one human arm bone? If it had been a burial site there should have been more than one.

I have personally looked at a great many relics found in the northeast woodlands. In fact I have examined the remains of over 500 prehistoric vessels. The pottery here was quite distinct. The decorating was executed in a much more precise fashion. A cross hatch design was lightly etched into the rim shards. This is totally unheard of in our area.

Also highly suspect is a slightly modified stone that is without question a human head fetish. This stone is light weight and brown. It has smaller stones set naturally set in where the mouth, nose and ear would be. The ear stone is notched. There was no stone in place by nature where the eye should have been, but you can still see the residue of an eye symbol that had been drawn on this face stone and was found about 15 feet from the image stone, laying on a pile of flint flakes that resembled a primitive altar. The back of the fetish is hollowed out for some unknown purpose.

I could find no belief or support from the professional archaeological community in Michigan—in fact all I found was ridicule. It did not seem to matter that the events had been witnessed by many people who could bear out the truth.

My quest for understanding lead me to write to the Early Sites Research Center in Rowley, Mass. Archaeological Director, James P. Whittall read my letter and at long last I had found someone to take me seriously. His reply was heartening.

Mr. Whittall said in his letter that, "Certainly the lettering is familiar and the symbols represent sun, moon. It is possible that this was someone's talisman, but with the unusual nature of the appearance of the markings I would suggest it is from a shaman's kit. Strange artifacts of this nature do show up all over the world, though most are inclined to think their reality is yet to be understood. It certainly was recovered in the right context."

There were many time when I would walk into my little museum and all the relics we had found would be dry, yet the image stone would be dripping wet. It seemed to attract people to it in a curious way, just as it did with me in the beginning. By far there are many more beautiful pieces in my collection Indian artifacts. Yet invariably people will come in and pick up this particular stone only to then be amazed at the story behind it. Some people claim that when they pick up the stone their fingers have a tingling sensation. I have experienced that same sensation many times myself.

I have tried to come up with some logical explanation for the appearance of the symbols, yet I can find none. As was suggested by Mr. Whittall, I believe that all indications point to the image stone as having been a shaman's amulet. It could be that someone endowed with strong powers could have

"charged" this stone with a message to be delivered up to its finder? If this is the case then how terribly sad that it should fall into my hands rather than a person who might have understood the communication.

To the North American Indian stones were extremely powerful and they figured prominently in their religious beliefs and ceremonies. This great significance of stones is easy to understand when you consider that they hunted their food with stone tipped arrow and spear shafts, chopped their wood for fires with stone axes, smoked their tobacco from stone pipes, used stones to process their foods and herbs, and so on.

The summer following my recovery of the image stone from my back yard I happened across a book by a Sioux medicine man named John (Fire) Lame Deer. In his book, "Lame Deer Seeker of Visions" (Simon and Schuster/1972) he spoke of stones which bear messages.

Lame Deer said, "A more modern word for rock is inyan. Inyan Wasicun Wakan is our Indian name for Moses. Indian medicine men, too, find round stones on the hilltops, which they bring down with them and use to cure people. And these stones bear a hidden message, which they sometimes reveal to us, invisible writing for those who read with their hearts. The old medicine men used to talk to stones and were able to communicate with them.

There were those shamans who were very skilled in the use of the stones and were often called to heal the sick using the sacred stones. As a rule people were invited to come and witness the healing to be performed. But if you did not believe in the power of the stone then it was best not to throw caution to the wind, harm could come to the disbeliever.

In a very old book whose author's name has been forgotten, the ceremony is described.

"The sick person filled a pipe, which he gave to the medicine man. After smoking it the man was tightly bound with thongs, even his fingers and toes being interlaced with sinews like those of which bow strings are made, after which he was firmly tied in a hide. The tent was dark, and the medicine-man sang songs addressed to the sacred stones; he sang also his own dream songs. Strange sounds were heard in the darkness and objects were felt to be flying through the air. Voices of animals were speaking. One said, "My grandchild, you are very sick, but I will cure you. Frequently a buffalo came, and those who did not believe in the sacred stones were kicked by the buffalo or struck by a flying stone or bundle of clothing. At last the medicine man called, "Hasten, make a light!" Dry grass, which was ready was placed on the fire. In its light the man was seen wedged between the poles near the top of the tipi, with all the restraining cords cast from him.

The Sioux believed that every man needed a stone to help him because they were holy. Lame Deer told of two types, one of which reminded me of my own image stone. Lame Deer described two kinds of stones that were good as medicine stones. They were pebbles, one type was as white as ice. The second type is an ordinary stone that by its character compels you to pick it up. This second type was like my stone.

Again, among the Sioux, Tunkan or the stone god is the most ancient of deities. He is the hardest and he is creation.

Sacred stones virtually dot the landscape of North America.

To the Indian, respect seems to have been heaped upon those objects which seemed slightly out of the ordinary in shape. Perhaps these had a more powerful manitou.

As an example in 1670 a stone idol was discovered by two priests near Lake Erie. The Indians of the region believed that stone overseer had control over navigation of the lake. Sacrifices were made to the stone whenever travel was to be conducted on the lake.

Mr. Bela Hubbard in the *Michigan Pioneer Collections* (Vol.3, page 649) reported the following account from 1837 of what he found near the mouth of the Kawkawlin River in 1837, "Upon a swelling knoll, overlooking the bay, in the midst of a tract of country from which all timber had been burned, was a spot which seemed to have been dedicated to an evil Manitou. Here an altar was erected, composed of two large stones which were covered with propitiatory offerings bits of tobacco, pieces of tin, flint, and such articles, of little value to the Indians, as, with religious philosophy, he dedicates to his Manitou."

In chapter one I told about a Late Woodland village site named Old Van Etten Creek where I have done extensive excavations. On one occasion I unearthed a small pile of fire cracked rocks. There were seventeen rocks, all neatly piled. At the time it made no sense to me at all. Now however this is recognizable to me as having been a small altar, or a "Manitou personnel.

Ephraim S. Williams in the *Michigan Pioneer and Historical Collection* spoke of such sacred objects. He said, "Nearly every Indian has discovered such an object in which he places special confidence, of which he most frequently thinks, and to which he sacrifices more zealously than to the Great Spirit. They call these things their Manitou personnel but the proper Ojibway word is said to be Nigouimes, which means My Hope. One calls a tree, another a stone or rock His Hope. Thus for instance, on the mainland opposite La Pointe there is an isolated boulder and huge, erratic block which the Voyageurs call le rocher. This rocher de Otamigan is in a swamp near one of the voyageurs resting places. There is also quoted here the legend of Tamigan and how he selected this rock for his manito: The Indian never goes past it without laying some tobacco on the rock as a sacrifice and often goes expressly to pay worship to it."

There is an unusual invocation to a stone god written of in the *Jesuit Relations 1664-65*. The Relations tell of an image of "black bronze" as described

A jigsaw of pottery, this 12 x 7 reconstruction seemed to act as a catalyst in the unusual first appearance of symbols on the stone.

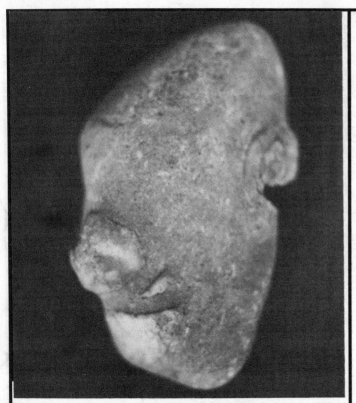

Human head fetish, shown here in profile. Look closely, and you can see where the eye was drawn in. The ear stone is notched. The back is concave and served perhaps a ritual use.

in the journal of Father Claude Allouez on his voyage into the Outaouac country.

The Relations tell, "There is observed in those regions of the Ottawas, a kind of idolatry which is rather unusual. They have a grotesque image of black bronze, one foot in height, which was found in the country, and to which they give a beard like a European's, although the savages themselves are beardless. There are certain fixed days for honoring this statue with feasts, games, dances and even with prayers, which are addressed to it with diverse ceremonies. Among them is one which, although ridiculous in itself, is yet remarkable in that it embraces a kind of sacrifice. All the men, one after another, approach the statue and, in order to pay homage with tobacco, offer it their pipes that it may smoke. But as the idol cannot avail itself of the offer, they smoke in its stead, blowing into its face the tobacco smoke, which they have in their mouths, which is regarded as a mode of offering incense and performing sacrifice."

There is little doubt that copper is being referred to here as black bronze, and the native copper in Michigan's upper peninsula is often in a matrix of rock.

As the years have passed and the Indian race has become subdued and relegated to specific areas so has the number of sacred stones diminished. To a great extent their power seems to be gone unless you are one who is enlightened to power possibly being there. As shown with the "image stone" I found, not all rocks have lost theirs powers, and in some cases, such as mine, the rocks reveal their power in a very graphic way.

Chapter Four: Ches-A-Kee Men and the Shaking Tent Rite

One of the most unusual and unexplainable of Indian religious rites in the north east woodland is that of the shaking tent. This is where the relationship between shaman and spirit attains its highest degree of sophistication. This is where the village can come into direct communication with the chief spirits in which they believe. Not a great deal has been written about this rite which is truly an enigma. It has not been that many years past that a conjurer visited the Mikado Indian Reservation near Mikado, Michigan. This was a truly eye opening experience which will form the basis of this chapter. First though, lets take a look at the shaking tent rites in general.

In the old days when this rite was performed very special care was taken in the erection of the shaking tent. Specific woods were used for the poles and no variation was allowed.

The tent has been described as being about

four feet in diameter.

About four feet above the ground a hoop was attached. A man would stand inside of this hoop and then slide a second hoop, which was smaller, over the top of the poles. This second hoop was then fixed securely in place.

This tepee-like cone frame was then covered over with canvas in historic times and with animal furs in prehistory. Though no mention is made of it in modern record I am sure it must have been a specific animal skin or skins that were used. The covering was lastly anchored firmly into the ground with stakes.

It has been hinted by Regina Flannery in her paper, *The Shaking Tent Rite Among The Montagnais of James Bay*, that before the actual rite began the conjurer spent his time in deep meditation. What these meditations were can only be imagined, but safely it can be said that it was probably on the spirits who enter the lodge during the ceremony.

The spirits who entered the tent differed from area to area depending on the belief of the local tribe. Perhaps it is the names that differed for the entity was essentially the same as near as can be determined.

The chief spirit of the rite among the Montagnais was named Mistabeo. Part of his duty in this rite was to interpret for the other spirits.

Ms. Flannery related a story which illustrated that Mistabeo must have a sense of humor. Having been a witness to a particular ceremony she related: "On the night to which I refer a couple of other spirits had come into the tent before Mistabeo, who, when he arrived, excused himself on the grounds that he didn't know the shaking tent was to be played with that night and as he was a long ways off, it took him some time to get there. Incidentally he also remarked on the smallness of the tent."

As in the Midaywiwin rites, songs play an important part here. One first hears the Song of the Trees, which has to be interpreted as few it is said can understand the language of the trees. With the commencement of this song the tent begins to shake gently, and does not hold still throughout the ceremony.

Other spirits who enter the tent include, Memegwecio, chief spirit of the clawed animals, and Mistcenaku who is the chief spirit of all things that are in the waters.

Something which differed between the rite at James Bay and the one at the Mikado Reservation is that at James Bay the audience was allowed to speak with the spirits. Many of the questions asked pertained of course to matters which were of direct import to the tribe; questions about hunting, fishing etc.

The conjurers role at James Bay seemed to be a minimal one with him not uttering any words. He was to kneel with his head bowed in reverence and nothing more.

Flannery related: "Once in a while Mistabeo would ask for a smoke, and a cigarette would be lighted and shoved under the tenting at the place where the conjurer had crawled in. Mistabeo was very humorous that night and made many remarks that elicited much laughter and comment from the on lookers. The remarks which drew the most merriment were those concerned with sex play."

Battles between spirits were not uncommon either. When one of these took place the tent would shake with violence as though a great battle were taking place inside. At the James Bay rite there was such a battle between Mistabeo and Memegwecio. Reportedly the audience could hear Mistabeo singing and Memegwecio puffing and blowing, scratching at the tent much in the manner a bear might have employed. On that night Mistabeo won the battle.

There was a general consensus among those who witnessed the rite at James Bay that the ceremonies in the older days were more powerful and meaningful. This was pretty much the way those attending the rite at Mikado felt, except there we were able to get a detailed account from an old conjurer.

The shaking tent rite is strictly a woodland area occurrence. As I said there are differences in the rite depending on where it is being practiced. In some groups, for example, the conjurer is tied up before entering the shaking tent. Some conjurers use a drum or rattle in the tent.

Within some tribes the shaking tent rite seems to have been the key to shamanistic rites but was not incorporated into their regular religious system. Other groups blended the rite into the rest of their religious beliefs, and why not, here was direct communication with the spirit world.

At the Mikado shaking tent rite our destination was an old building site the people of King's Corner Settlement called "John's Place." Here lay the charred and scattered remains of an old log building long ago burned to the ground. It was a pleasant mid-summer evening as we walked through the small orchard by the blackened timbers, some forty of us—a mixture of Indians and whites following an ancient path through the Michigan forest which has been carved deep by the footsteps of many that came before us.

Halting at last, we formed a rough circle around a conical structure of poles and bark some seven feet tall called a pineswigamik, as a young Ches-a-kee man entered and dropped to his knees.

We waited a few moments and nothing happened. It should have begun shaking the moment he entered, an Indian on looker muttered somewhat disappointedly. Others, both Indians and whites laughed rather loudly, as if to say the whole affair was foolishness. Many in this crowd were Christian Indians and felt what was being done was wrong and should not be taking place. Many whites did not believe in the spiritual powers of the Indians but had come with camera and notebook anyway to record the proceedings if only for the amusement value of it all.

The young man who entered the picturesque but crudely made lodge, looking not unlike a tepee but smaller, was in his mid twenties and was visiting the King's Corner Indian Settlement along with his father and elder Uncle from the Beren's River area of Upper Canada. Tall and well structured, the young man possessed graceful movement so characteristic of most Saulteaux. His father was rather fat however, and sat cross legged in the grass, his round face showing no emotion. The final Barens River Indian, the young man's uncle was in advanced age, slow and weak in his movement, with long white hair and deep creases in his leathery face and neck. He was a man of mystery. There were many things intriguing about him of which he spoke. His mind was razor sharp and he seemed to intuitively know what you were thinking, often answering your questions before they were asked. It had happened too many times to have just been chance. This fact had become readily apparent when he conversed at length on the following day.

He was a Ches-a-kee man, but for him no longer would Pawagawnack come. The powers are like a brightly burning fire at first. Then the fire grows dim with age. Finally the Pawagawnack will not come, he said. He was against his nephew trying to call the spirits, feeling his nephew was not a real Ches-a-kee man. The young man had never had the sequence of dream revelations necessary to make him a conjurer. For the old white haired man hobbling down the crooked trail nothing was right about this and he had stopped several times stating that he wished to go back to Alfred's, the place where they were staying, and begin the long trip back to his northern homeland. But the enthusiastic crowd had moved him onward.

Now very soon the ancient form of American Indian religion called conjuring would be taking place. Documents from the 18th and 19th century were somewhat convincing as to the manifestation of supernatural forces within the conjuring lodge. The events to happen, or not to happen, within the next few hours would shed some light on this.

The event would take place with some good background knowledge about the mechanics of conjuring. For the old Ches-a-kee man with the Anglo name of Simon Felix and the Indian name of Strikes-

the Post, had told about his lifetime of conjuring, of being directly in touch with the spirit world.

I had learned of Mikanack, of Pineswak and at least 30 more of these ghost helpers of the American Indian from this kind old man. He became a living link to the past. When he related the experiences of his own childhood in regards to the Ches-a-kee men, he knew it would take me back into the original religious world of the Indian before their life styles and beliefs were altered.

"It is not wrong for me to tell you everything about us. You are sincere and you should be told so you can tell others. Know there have been few great Ches-a-keee men in our history. The population of our people at any given time has been small and few are chosen by the Master Spirit of Conjuring to perform. There have been bad Ches-a-kee men, not so good ones, and there have been imposters. Put it all down on your paper so all people will know what we once were.

"As the professional white men claim, we are shamanist, this is true. But we are not ordinary shamans. Our extra powers to secure news about people who are hundreds of miles away, learn of events taking part in other parts of the country, know what will happen in the future, recover lost or stolen articles, tell hunters where the animal food is, abduct souls, cause sickness, mental disorder and death sets us apart from other types of medicine men.

"The professional white men who long ago came to our village to study us says most of our characteristic function is seership or clairvoyance. They are probably right in their interpretation of us and our powers but the words they use are not our words. What I am telling you is in our words, from the Indian mind and heart.

"We look the same as other Indians. There is no difference in our bodies, but our minds are different. Our ability to conjure is acquired by receiving certain powers which come in dreams while we are very young. Four dreams within a brief period of time, say, three weeks, creates the best Ches-a-kee men. Most have fewer dreams than this. The professional whites say a supernatural revelation occurs in certain select Indians. This is probably true. No one can predict who will become a Ches-a-kee man. No one can teach another to conjure. The very best Ches-a-kee men have had their first dream at about two years of age.

"I acquired my powers early. I was not more than six or seven years old. Even before entering the shaking lodge with my grandfather who was the greatest of Ches-a-kee men, several Pawaganack already had come to me but I did not know what they were. Though it was in the dead of winter my body was wet with sweat, I remember my legs jerking wildly. It was night and the fires in our stoves had burned down. To ward off the gathering cold I remember pulling my Hudson's Bay blanket around me more snugly. When there, on the edge of my blanket, before my eyes, danced four tiny little human like creatures. I remembered thinking they resembled sparks from burning tamarack wood. So bright were these brilliant little creatures that I could not long look directly at them. It was very strange but I was not afraid. It was real, not a dream, and I seemed to know beyond all doubt that something important was happening to me. Then they were gone. The following day my father told my grandfather what had happened to me. My grandfa-

ther promised then I would soon be taken into the shaking lodge with him to see the spirits.

"Not long after, my grandfather was called on to conjure by our people. A shirt, some teas and a box of buttons were placed before him. He stared intently for a few moments then picked the items up. The people knew then that he would conjure. It is always done that way.

"When the evening to conjure arrived my grandfather instructed my father to bring me to the lodge and let me look inside. My father did so, thrusting me inside the strange dwelling. My grandfather was kneeling on the boughs and the conjuring ceremony was in full swing with the lodge vibrating and shimmering. There was a great wind within the lodge making me shiver and my eyes water. I was in my fathers arms, thrust forward through the lodge opening with my face upward. It was another world in there, my young mind readily grasped the world within a world. Above my grandfather near the top of the lodge, were the strange little creatures I had seen. They swirled like bees. Tiny brilliant sparks with peculiar shapes, ever changing, sometimes human like, sometimes animal like. Whistling sounds filled the lodge, sounds like the human voice but shriller, sounds like rabbits squealing, crows cawing, deer snorting, sounds of thunderstorms, of the four winds.

"The following day my grandfather asked if his Pawaganack were what I had seen that night on the edge of my wool blanket. I told him that they were what I had seen. He then said I would have special powers when I grew up. He became stern. He instructed me to never play at conjuring and never to make a play lodge to conjure in. Children were never to mimic the activities of the Ches-a-kee men.

"The years passed and I obeyed him, never conjuring until I became a man. With fair results I helped the people of our village find food, cured many of the diseases that afflicted them, helped them find lost items, and I predicted the individual futures of many of them. But I was not regarded as a good Ches-a-kee man. The highlight of those first years as I remember them now in the dimness of fading memory was when Kadoebending came to me. This is the master of conjuring and is also known to my people as Azagizi-Iwe. It was a great event for it meant that I would become the best of Ches-a-kee men.

"Yet it was only through my grandfathers death that I felt the real power coming to me. I always remember, conjuring is the gift of the thunder god and the home of the master is located in the west where the sun goes down. With my grandfathers passing many of his Pawaganack came to me and stayed with me. Then new ones came and the old ones doubled in power. They came out of the west, from the home of Pineswak, the Thunderbird, and all came down the path way of souls. Remember too, that this is the same path my grandfather used when he died and went to the land of the souls."

He sat among the green cedars by the little creek known as Rattlesnake with a soft wind bringing the sweet smell of the summer forest. The old man's eyes were watery and red, his speech was slow and strained, but he continued, his thoughts flowing gently like the clear water in the creek.

"It is not a good time for the Indians now. They lose the power and the old ways. They do not believe as strongly or go through the necessary rituals. The spirits lose faith in us. Even now as we talk my nephew who will conjure drinks beer and wine at Alfred's. It is wrong to take the powers so lightly.

"When Indians had control of their lives in the long ago even the poles selected for the shaking lodge were important. The master of conjuring, Kadoebending, instructs each new conjurer when and how to construct the lodge. Methods varied with the Ches-a-kee men, but my lodge had to have seven poles of seven species of trees; birch, ash, maple, oak, cedar, pine and spruce. Nothing was accomplished haphazardly. Everything was done as prescribed by the master spirit of conjuring. Remember in knowing about Indians, everything has a master for the species. Make no mistake, there is also a master for every group of non-living things, such as rocks. And above all these in power and importance is the greatest creator who no one has seen but who all must answer to.

"Always the bottom of the shaking lodge was covered with fresh cut spruce boughs. The side of the lodge was covered loosely with birch bark or reed mats. The covering material was not solidly applied or over lapped to shed the weather like a regular tepee home. From outside people could see inside through the cracks, hear the voices of the spirits, and often see them.

"No Ches-a-kee man ever built his own lodge. Two men, no more than three, had to this job. The lodge had to be built before sun down. Conjuring was always done in the evening. Once used, the lodge was taken down and could never be used again. A hole was dug and all things were buried.

"My clothes had to be cleaned before and after conjuring. The lodge had to be built on a clean spot of ground where no one had even spit and no village dogs had urinated or defecated.

"Before conjuring I -would circle -the lodge clock wise, feeling the forces of the spirits, letting them know I was ready. Then I would enter my lodge, and it would begin to shake, slowly at first, then more violently with up to three feet gyrations at the top when all my Pawaganack were present.

"Mikinack, the turtle is the chief spirit of the shaking lodge for all Ches-a-kee men and is directly responsible to the Great Spirit. Mikinack is a messenger in all performances and also interprets for some Pawaganack who often speak in languages we do not know.

"The best Ches-a-kee men can bring thirty two Pawaganack into the shaking lodge. Five are part animal—part human forms which the professional white men call anthropomorphic. Four are miniature humanoid, one of which is Windigo who can be conjured into a giant by some Ches-a-kee men. The others, the greatest number, are masters of the animal species which number twenty three. It must be remembered that Pawaganack do not look exactly animal.

"In the shaking lodge only Mickinack, the turtle spirit came low, down by my body, sometimes touching the boughs I knelt upon. All other Pawaganack stayed near the top of the lodge where the whirlwinds made humming sounds. Some sat upon the lodge hoops. All were like brilliant sparks, as I mentioned before.

"Ches-a-kee men can not perform too frequently. Conjuring can not be done for fun. There must be a real need. Often the conjuring ordeal is too exhausting. The helping spirits disturb too greatly the Ches-a-kee man's soul.

"Other than being liked and respected by the people, there is no gain for us. Ches-a-kee men are the poorest in the tribe. We do not do it for gain, though we do receive things. The people come to us in times of great need; sick, disturbed, afraid. They lay a few things before us, some tea or coffee, maybe a shirt. If the Ches-a-kee man picks up the offering it means he will conjure. We receive little of personal value for ourselves from conjuring. But the prestige value is strong. We are respected and highly regarded.

"Put it all down on paper for our truth must be recorded so white will know. The spirits speak directly to the conjurer or in his presence, never through him. This is the very oldest form of conjuring. It is the true form. The new form of conjuring, speaking through the conjurer is not as old nor is it as good. This form is where much fakery exists. People laugh and scoff when they see fake conjurers perform this way and do not believe any conjurer has the power to summon the spirits.

"We never go into trances or slip into spiritual states of ecstasy like some say and write about us. The white professionals called anthropologists say that conjuring is nearly absent in the New England area. This is true for only the Cree, Montagnais, Naskapi, Ojibwa and Saulteaux are the Ches-a-kee men. Outside of what is known as the woodland area the shaking lodge is performed only by the plains Cree and Cheyenne. They knew about it from us, through marriage and by being prisoners taken during warfare.

"Women seldom become conjurers. Men are natural links between the spirit world and this one. Women having this exceptional supernatural gift may conjure, however, following their final moon tepee visit (following menopause) for they then are more like men. Blue-Robed Cloud-Woman was an excellent conjurer from the Lake Superior country. My grandfather often spoke of her great powers and, of her personally with great admiration and affection.

"Animal-human metamorphosis, transmigration, reincarnation are some of the terms attributed to what we do by professional white men who came and studied us. It is their words, but it is fair to say the words described the results from our powers accurately.

"We are good and we do good but there are some things Ches-a-men do that are bad. This must be told too. Conjurers sometimes summon to their lodge the soul of a rival conjurer. Then each man summons all of his Pawaganack. It then is a struggle to the death. Christian missionaries and Christian Indians do not like this. Also, Ches-a-kee men will at times consult the master for the spirit of the dead, then send his Pawaganack to the land of the dead to retrieve a soul to put back in a recently dead body. They heap scorn upon us and say we do work of the devil. This is not fair for we do good things. By picking out a few bad things we do it helped missionaries turn many Indians to Christianity when we did these things.

"Much of a similar nature has been written to discredit us. Some have said we are fakes, that our powers are not real. They have said that we are but jugglers, clever magicians. Some of us do resort to fakery, especially the young men who try hard. Often a good Ches-a-kee man increases his powers by grasping firmly one of the poles of his lodge. This makes the lodge shake even more. It makes the wind rotate more and the spirits come sooner and in greater number. This has lead many people to believe that the Chesa-kee man is shaking the lodge himself. It is not true of course. As previously stated, the poles of the shaking lodge are buried as much as two feet in the ground. Often in the dead of winter when a real need to call the spirit helpers arises, a lodge may be set up in a log cabin with hole bored through the wooden floor to hold the poles up. Often the shaking lodge is set up within a tepee in the winter or within a multiple family dwelling. An examination of the outside of any conjuring lodge readily discloses its firmness. The lodge can not be budged, often by several men who try to shake it with all their might.

"Long ago, Ches-a-kee man took up the challenge of these disbelievers. We have willingly displayed our powers for the professional whites who studied us, for the priests and preachers that came to give us a new religion, and for the men who write books and professional papers about us. On death bed, every conjurer ever questioned by whites who study such things, stated that the powers were real. Even those eventually converted to Christianity never denied the existence of their Pawaganack.

"Many times, preachers and priests prayed for us at ceremonies, seeing with their own eyes the work of our Pawaganack. They said it was not the work of God but of the devil. If the devil does good work then it was the devil. To prove our powers to the disbelievers Ches-a-kee men let themselves be wrapped with blankets, then tied tightly with ropes, then thrown in their lodges. The lodges would still shake the moment their bodies hit the spruce boughs. When the Pawaganack came, many moved away in fear, leaving, vowing to never attend such affairs again. With more than thirty people present I was wrapped with a fish net and had my hands bound behind me. On my knees, I waddled into the lodge. It began to shake and all my Pawaganack came. For two hours the spirits gave advice and solved problems for my people. Then I crawled out, the same way I had entered. to the astonishment of all disbelievers present.

"At Leech Lake, Minnesota, with almost fifty people present, a Ches-a-kee man named, Sun-Climbing-The-Sky, had four conjuring lodges built. In these lodges he tossed articles of his clothing. When he entered the fourth lodge all four began to shake. To our own people, we Ches-a-kee men have proven our powers since time began. For the whites we have proven it as long as they have been here. We do not have to prove it no more. I could tell you many more things, but it is all you need to know to basically understand our powers." The crowd had quieted down. We had been standing and setting around the conjuring lodge now for about half an hour. The lessening of the noise was to better hear the sounds beginning to come from the lodge, not due to any great reverence for the ceremony. "Its plainly the voice of a young man," an Indian woman said. Others agreed. I thought it was too.

The old man left, throwing up his hands as he moved slowly back up the trail. I waited for a few minutes more and then hurried to catch up with him. "We will start back home tomorrow," he said stopping to regain his breath. Darkness was coming on casting dark shadows around us. "Web-en-dag-en was a good Ches-a-kee man. You had him right here in this village. Web-en-dag-en means pocket. You people called him Charlie Pocket. He had only one leg. It was off at the knee and he carved a fine wooden one out of ash wood. One side of his face had been blown off. He was old when he settled here, but he still had some powers left. He cured the pox here. He saved the settlement. These people wouldn't be here now if it wasn't for the power of Wab-en-dag-en. But its not a good time for Ches-a-kee men anymore."

Chapter Five: Bearwalker and the Evil in the Northeast Woodland

There exists in the north east woodland culture an evil which is as inherent to the woodland as is the shaking tent. It is an evil which strikes fear into the hearts of many Indians yet today, but especially

Omaha sub-chief Standing Bear, a representative of the Indian peoples, at the Jardin d'Acclimation de Paris. Photography funded by Prince Roland Bonaparte, c. 1883.

those of the Chippewa culture. The evil is known as the Bearwalker. Like the Midaywiwin and the shaking tent, the Bearwalker finds its roots in prehistory though it still actively spins its mystical web today. The Bearwalker goes by the Indian name of Mock-wa-mosa and is said to be the Indian equivalent of white man's witchcraft.

In a video taped interview with Chief John Nahgahgwon of the Mikado Indian Reservation, the chief spoke with some apprehension, of his personal memories of the Mock-wa-mosa.

Chief Nahgahgwon explained that the Bearwalker used their powers to settle grudges. It is, however, a grudge settler which reacts only upon the Indians and cannot be turned on whites. The practitioners are said to be very sly indeed. In modern times cult members are known to pose as good Christian church goers but do the Mock-wa-mosa on the side.

The power imbued in the modern practitioners comes down from ancient times and is passed from one generation to another. The manner of transfer is quite simple but varies according to circumstances. When a practitioner feels that he or she is near death's door they call to themselves a kinsman and simply tell that person, "I have something for you." The power cannot be refused and the power must be used. Through the use of the Mock-wa-mosa powers the possessor must kill at least one person per year or the power will turn on its possessor and kill him.

Another method of transfer of power was related by Archie Megenuph from Michigan's upper peninsula to Richard M. Dorson in his book, "Bloodstoppers and Bearwalkers."

Megenuph related, "You can catch one if you have the right medicine. You chew and sprinkle the medicine on yourself, and you wait for the bearwalk. Then you put your arms around it, and it is all naked, except for a string of beads around the neck. Then it asks you to let it go, promises you anything, to suckle you, to teach you the bearwalk. Then if you let it go, you go and learn from it, like from a professor. They caught one here once that way. I'd like to be a bearwalk. If you shoot them you can't ever catch them. You can't bring them to your premises, they must always go home to die. You don't find anything when you shoot them either, but they die off some distance."

Chief Nahgahgwon related that among other things, the person with this power can transform themselves to any shape they so desire.

Most frequently the choice is a bear. In this form they stalk forth to revenge wrongs done to themselves or kinsmen, and they have tremendous power indeed. If in this form they even pass by an innocent bystander, that person (unless of extremely strong constitution) is knocked unconscious by the sheer power concentrated in this being.

Alec Philemon was a personal witness to this incredible concentration of power by which even future events can sometimes be predicted. Philemon related, "When I was thirteen, fourteen, I was going with my mother and sister to visit a sick woman. We left there about eleven o'clock in the evening, and I saw the fire right on the main road (which goes to the church now). My mother and sister fell right over. I caught my mother. She said; That must have been a bearwalk, it was to much for us. Then she said, "You'll live the longest. My sister fell first, and she died first too. They both died of the flu in 1918. That woman we visited—about a half an hour after we got home we heard the bell ring, that woman was dead."

As illustrated in the above story, brilliant lights are often times associated with the bearwalker. When a person transforms to the bear and walks upright through the forests in search of its victims the beast is ablaze with brilliant light. One of the more common shapes to be assumed is that of a huge fireball. Chief Nahgahgwon recalled one

evening watching the barn by his house, "I remember one going down by the woods by my house, you could just see the trees all light up."

The chief was quick to point out that there is protection, though it varies from that detailed by Megenuph earlier. The chief said that whether you are an innocent or the sought after party, if you possess a little slyness yourself, when you have spotted the Mockwa-mosa coming down the trail you must double back. Take a pinch of sand from the trail where it has walked and place this in your lip. It is said that kills the power of the beast.

At the Mikado Reservation there lived a woman practitioner. Her name need not be mentioned. At any rate, another elderly Indian has told that he and his brother were walking through the woods one day and they saw a bearwalker coming down the path. They got sly and hid off the side of the path. They leapt upon the beast as it passed. The

Omaha Chief Yellow Smoke, a representative of the Indian peoples, at the Jardin d'Acclimation de Paris. Photography funded by Price Roland Bonaparte, c. 1883.

beast was spitting fire and fighting like crazy but finally gave up. The monster turned into the woman mentioned above and begged for her release which they granted her.

A lady, Nancy Picard, of French Indian descent related that her father died on the night of January 14, 1914. She recalled that she and various other members of her family saw the Mock-wa-mosa light hanging in the woods in the back of the house. She said that it looked like a round ball of light, and that some of the family went to investigate. They were so overtaken by chills that they were forced to turn back. But they all knew it was the power.

Nancy also told that a person who has the power can take all forms, but the favored forms were the bear or the owl. Light generally is present with these manifestations.

I am going to quote again from Nancy Picard, and pay attention in particular to the description of the ball of light. Nancy is speaking about a young girl who took very sick. She related to Mr. Dorson, "People watched all day to keep anyone away. Every night they'd see a light hanging in line with the trees; it would dance around like a flame. An old woman,

Mrs. Elijah, tried to get in, time and time again, when the body was in the house. Dan borrowed money to go to Odanah, Wisconsin, to contact a person who had power to counteract the evil. He was afraid the whole family would be wiped out. That new medicine was supposed to kill the effect of the original dose. It was quite a notorious affair. Even the white people in the county were interested."

Remember the lights and pay attention to that through the rest of these accounts because we will come back to these later.

Some practitioners were easily picked out of a crowd. They were said to have eyes that were all bloodshot, looked at you cross eyed, and could never look you directly in the eyes.

Mrs. Elijah had quite a reputation surrounding her. One individual in speaking of her claimed that she had nearly been witched by the elderly Mock-wa-mosa. This lady grabbed hold of Mrs. Elijah's arm to give her a lift, and her arm was suddenly wracked with pain. Subsequently over the next few weeks the arm became numb.

The expertise of a shaman was necessary and one was called in. He made a sort of plaster from

herbs and roots which was held on the arm for about a half an hour. The lady swears that this peculiar poultice extracted feathers, hairs and beads from the afflicted appendage.

Mrs. Elijah died a death that sounds as though it was befitting someone who practiced such evil forces. She is said to have gone crazy with all the mischief she had caused and even got to the point of trying to irritate the whites. The night of her death it is said she went to a pool room and wanted to sleep there on the pool table. Her son-in-law put her in a shack to sleep but she left that on her own and went out into the woods. They say that her "guts" were dropping out of her and she hung them on a tree and that is how she died.

When she was found she was buried on the spot with no coffin.

When the bearwalker makes someone die the family goes to the grave on the fourth night to protect the corpse, and this also provides another opportunity to end the evil power. The Mock-wa-mosa was required to go to the grave four days after in order to get back the medicine she used.

On one such occasion a group of family saw the fireball coming. They were scared and all fainted save for one old man, who by the way died at ninety eight. He reportedly glanced up and saw the bear stomping on the grave and spitting fire. He is said to have grabbed hold of the bear and it vanished, in his grips was an old woman bearwalker. She was said to have buckskin bags all over her, and that she had a bearskin hide on her. It is also believed that whoever

the bearwalker kills, it must take a toe or a finger to put into one of these bags.

The desecration of the corpse was further borne out by Archie Megenuph who related the following in, "Bloodstoppers and Bearwalkers," "If you don't have the right medicine they put you to sleep even if you have a gun, and walk right past you to the patient. It's as if you were paralyzed. They go every fourth night and on the sixteenth the patient is finished. You can be in a room with your wife, and you'll fall asleep when the bearwalk comes in. You can hear him go out. They can take any shape, fowl or animal or insect. That grasshopper you kick may be it. On the fourth night after they kill the patient, they go to the grave, and you can hear the carcass rise right up out of the casket, and they cut off the fourth or fifth finger and the tongue tip and put it with their victim set." The eye, finger or tongue tip must come from the right side of the victim. If for some reason the Mock-wa-mosa cannot get to the grave it will die after a period of four months.

One last eye witness account is on my desk which involves the mysterious light phenomenon connected with the Mock-wa-mosa. Alec Philemon told that, "There were three of us, one a couple years older, coming back from Bark river at nighttime. We saw a flash coming from behind us. The older fellow said; It's a bearwalk, lets get it. I'll stand on the other side of the road and you stand on this side.

"We stood there and waited. I saw it about 50 feet away from US. It looked like a bear, but every time he would breath you could see a gust of flames. My chum fell over in a faint. When the bearwalk all the ground wave, like when you walk on soft mud or on moss. He was goin' where he was goin'."

I asked you to pay particular attention to the description of the "ball" lights. The north east woodlands have always been particularly prone to UFO sightings. Many of these sightings match or are similar to phenomena associated with the Mock-wa-mosa. Of course, not all UFO activity in the large area of the United States and Canada can be attributed to this, but it is quite possible that some can be. After all, the bearwalk is still commonly practiced but is unknown to most whites. When the ethereal light is seen the native mind would attribute it to the bearwalk, however, UFO would promptly flash into the minds of most others.

This calls to mind a time when my wife, then fiancee, Kathy and I were driving a desolate stretch of Old U.S. 23 near Tuttle Marsh. Tuttle Marsh is a good place to stay away from, particularly at night.

We were driving along and observed a bright flash of red light come from the north, heading south then arching down into the woods where it hung briefly before disappearing. Not being familiar at that time with the Indian culture I thought right away of UFO's.

In 1966 the Native Americans may have been setting back while having quite a laugh at the expense of the general American populace which was anxious and nearing panic.

In 1966 the United States was undergoing a truly large UFO flap that seemed centered in the north east. You could not turn on a TV or radio without hearing about the phenomena. Particularly affected was Michigan and New York. Perhaps you remember? At that time in our travel through history, the government felt people were incapable of hearing the truth about UFO's (come to think of it, 26 years later not much has changed in that respect).

The government, being pressed for an explanation from all around, hired Dr. J. Allan Hynek to play the dupe for them. He announced to the world that the ignorant folk up in the north east were seeing nothing but swamp gas, an explanation that was rejected by most of the thinking public. No satisfactory explanation has ever been published as to what was really being sighted.

Rather than something from outer space, perhaps it was something quite down to earth which finds its origins in the ancient powers of the north east woodlands.

Let me relate to you one sighting of hundreds that sound in modern terms very much like the balls of light associated with the Mock-wa-mosa.

It was on March 20, 1966, in south east Michigan. The Mannor family was sitting down to Sunday dinner in their two-story, white farmhouse on McGuiness Road. A hollow and a creek separated the house from a 300 acre swamp. Present that evening were Mr. and Mrs. Manor, two of their married daughters and their husbands, and Ronald, Frank Mannor's 19 year old son. They were already seated at the table when the dogs began howling in the yard.

Mort Young, in his book *UFO Top Secret,*

(Essandess/1967) best captured the mood of excitement surrounding the events. Mort reported, "Mannor went outside to quiet the dogs but they were in a frenzy. A ball of fire arched across the sky. Mannor decided it was a shooting star—until it halted its plunge in midair, just above a cluster of trees in the swamp. Lights flickered at either end of the fiery ball. Then it plummeted behind the trees, a ruddy glow marking its location.

"The rest of the family joined Mannor outside. They could see the faint glow, see the brush painted red by its reflection. Without waiting to take flashlights or guns, Frank and Ronnie Mannor started down the gentle rise to the swamp. They knew every inch by heart having hunted deer in it.

"Frank and Ronnie Mannor plodded through knee-high muck, barely able to see where they put their feet. Ahead, a flickering glow silhouetted a knoll.

"At eye level, 500 yards in front of them, a football-shaped grey object the length of a car shimmered in the darkness. It rested on a cushion of haze, about eight feet above the mud. The object suddenly burned bloody red and then the lights blinked out."

The incidents of that spring and summer will long be etched in the minds of many. One should not over look the possibility that these sightings have their origins right here on good old planet earth.

Speaking of origins, and since this chapter has been dealing with the evil encompassed in the

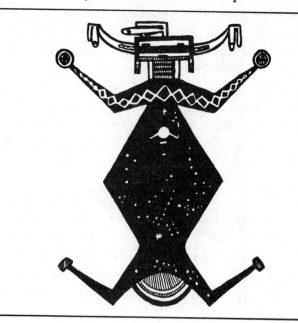

40

Mock-wa-mosa or bearwalker, it would be interesting to look at how the American Indians of the north east view the origins of evil.

Much is owed to the famous ethnologist, Henry R. Schoolcraft, for he is directly responsible for many Indian legends being written down and preserved for us. Without these our understanding of their culture would indeed be lacking.

In his 1851 work, *History of the American Indian,* Schoolcraft presented a story titled, "Machinito, The Evil Spirit." Let's look at how evil began.

Chemanitou, being the master of life, at one time became the origin of a spirit, that has ever since caused himself and all others of his creation a great deal of disquiet. His birth was owing to an accident. This is how it happened:

"Metowac, or as the white people now call it, Long Island, was originally a vast plain, so level and free from any kind of growth, that it looked like a portion of the great sea that had suddenly been made to move back and let the sand below appear, which was the case in fact.

"Here it was that Chemanitou used to come and sit, when he wished to bring any new creation to life. The place being spacious and solitary, the water upon every side, he had not only room enough, but was free from interruption.

"It is well known that some of these creations were of very great size, so that very few could live in the same place, and their strength made it difficult for Chemanitou even to control them; for when he gave them certain elements, they had the use of the laws that govern these elements, till it was his will to take them back to himself. Accordingly it was the custom of Chemanitou when he wished to try the effect of these creatures, to set them in motion upon the island of Metowac, and if they did not please him, he took the life out before they were suffered to escape. He would set up a mammoth or other large animal in the center of the island and build him up with great care, somewhat in the manner that a cabin or a canoe is made.

"Even to this day may be found traces of what had been done here in former years, and the manner in which the earth sometimes sinks down (even wells fall out at the bottom here) shows that this island is nothing more than a great cake of earth, a sort of platter laid upon the sea for the convenience of Chemanitou who used it as a table upon which he might work, never having designed it for anything else; the margin of the Chatiemac, (the stately swan) or Hudson river, being better suited to the purposes of habitation.

"When the master of life wished to build up an elephant or mammoth he placed four cakes of clay upon the ground at the proper distances, which were molded into shape, and became the feet of the animal.

"Now sometimes these were left unfinished; and to this day the green tussocks, to be seen like islands about the marshes, show where these cakes of clay had been placed.

"As Chemanitou went on with his work, the Neebanawbaigs (or water spirits), the Puck-wud-jinnies (fairies), and indeed all the lesser manitous, used to come and look on, and wonder what it would be and how it would act.

"When the animal was quite done, and had dried a long time in the sun, Chemanitou opened a place in the side and entering in, remained there many days.

"When he came fourth the creature began to shiver and sway from side to side, in such a manner as he shook the whole island for many leagues. If his appearance pleased the master of life he was suffered, and it was generally found that these animals plunged into the sea upon the north side of the island and disappeared in the great forests beyond.

"Now at one time Chemanitou was a very long while building an animal of such great bulk that it looked like a mountain upon the center of the island; and all the manitous, from all parts, came to see what it was. The Puck-wud-jinnies especially made themselves very merry, capering behind its great ears, sitting within its mouth, each perched upon a tooth, and running in and out of the sockets of the eyes, thinking Chemanitou, who was finishing off other parts of the animal, could not see them.

"But he can see right through everything he has made. He was glad to see them so lively, and it was left upon the island, or work table of Chemanitou, till its great weight caused it to break through, and sinking partly down it stuck fast, the head and tail holding it in such a manner as to prevent it from going down.

"Chemanitou then lifted up a piece of the back and found it made a very good cavity into which the old creations, which failed to please him might be thrown.

"He sometimes amused himself by making creatures very small and active with which he desported awhile, and finding them of very little use in the world, and not so attractive as the little Vanishers, he would take out the life, holding it in himself, and then cast them into the cave made by the body of the unfinished animal. In this way great quantities of very odd shapes were heaped together in Roncomcomon, or, Place of Fragments.

"He was always careful to first take out the life.

"One day the master of life took two pieces of clay and molded them into two large feet, like those of a panther. He did not make four—there were only two.

"He stepped his own feet into them and found they tread very light and springy, so that he might go with great speed, and yet make no noise.

"Next he built up a very tall pair of legs in the shape of his own, and made them walk about a while—he was pleased with the motion. Then followed a round body, covered with large scales, like an alligator.

"He now found the figure doubling forward, and he fastened a long black snake, that was gliding by, to the back part of the body and let it wind itself about a nearby sapling, which held the body upright and made a very good tail.

"The shoulders were broad and strong, like those of the buffalo, and covered with hair—the neck thick and short, and full at the back.

"Thus far Chemanitou had worked with little thought, but when he came to the head he thought a long while.

"He took a round ball of clay into his lap and worked it over with great care. While he thought, he patted the ball on the top, which made it very broad and low; for Chemanitou was thinking of the panther feet and the buffalo neck. He remembered the Puck-wudjennies playing in the eye sockets of the great unfinished animal, and he bethought him to set the eyes out, like those of a lobster, so that the animal might see upon every side.

"He made the forehead broad and full, but low; for here was to be the wisdom of the forked tongue, like that of the serpent, which should be in his mouth. He should see all things and know all things. Here Chemanitou stopped, for he saw that he had never thought of such a creation before, one with but two feet, a creature who should stand upright, and see upon every side.

"The jaws were very strong with ivory teeth, and gills upon either side, which arose and fell whenever breath passed through them. The nose was like the beak of a vulture. A tuft of porcupine quills made the scalp-lock.

"Chemanitou held the head out the length of his arm, and turned it first upon one side and then upon the other. He passed it rapidly through the air and saw the gills rise and fall, the lobster eyes whirl around, and the vulture nose look keen.

"Chemanitou became very sad; yet he put the head upon the shoulders.

It was the first time he had made an upright figure. It seemed the idea of a man.

"It was now nearly night, the bats were flying through the air, and the roar of the wild beasts began to be heard. A gusty wind swept in from the ocean, and passed over the island of Metowac, casting the light sand to and fro. A heavy scud was skimming along the horizon, while higher up in the sky was a dark thick cloud, upon the verge of which the moon hung for a moment, and then was shut in.

A panther came by and stayed a moment, with one foot raised and bent inward while he looked up at the image, and smelled the feet that were like his own.

"A vulture swooped down with a great noise of its wings, and made a dash at the beak, but Chemanitou held him back.

"Then came the porcupine, and the lizard, and the snake, each drawn by its kind in the image.

"Chemanitou veiled his face for many hours, and the gusty wind swept by, but he did not stir.

"He saw that every beast of the earth seeketh its kind; and that which is like draweth its likeness unto himself.

"The Master of Life thought and thought. The idea grew into his mind that at sometime he would create a creature who should be made not after the things of the earth, but after himself.

"He should link this world to the spirit world, being made in the likeness of the Great Spirit, he should be drawn unto his likeness.

"Many days and nights, whole seasons—passed while Chemanitou thought upon these things. He saw all things.

Then the Master of Life lifted up his head; the stars were looking down upon the image, and a bat had alighted upon the forehead, great wings upon each side. Chemanitou took the bat and held out its whole leathery wings, (and every since the bat, when he rests, lets his body hang down) so that he could try them over the head of the image. He then took the life of the bat away and twisted off the body, by which means the whole thin part fell down over the head, and upon each side, making the ears, and a covering for the forehead like that of the hooded serpent.

"Chemanitou did not cut off the face of the image below, he went on and made a chin, and lips that were firm and round, that they might shut in the forked tongue, and the ivory teeth; and he knew that with the lips and the chin it would smile when life should be given to it.

"The image was now all done but the arms, and Chemanitou saw that with a chin it must have hands. He grew more grave.

"He had never given hands to any creature.

"He made the arms and the hands very beautiful, after the manner of his own.

"Chemanitou took no pleasure in his work nopw that was done, it was not good in his sight.

"He wished he had not given it hands; might it not, when trusted with life, might it not begin to create? Might it not thwart the plans of the Master of Life himself?

"He looked long at the image. He saw what it would do when life should be given it. He knew all things.

"He now put fire in the image; but fire is not life.

"He put fire within, and a red glow passed through and through it. The fire dried the clay of which it was made, and gave the image an exceedingly fierce aspect. It shone through the scales on the breast, and the gills and the bat-winged ears. The lobster eyes were like a living coal.

"Chemanitou opened the side of the image, but he did not enter. He had given it hands and a chin.

"It could smile like the manitous themselves.

"He made it walk all about the island of Metowac that he might see how it would act. This he did by means of his will.

"He now put a little life into it, but he did not take out the fire. Chemanitou saw the aspect of the creature would be very terrible, and yet that he could smile in such a manner that he ceased to be ugly. He thought much upon these things. He felt it would not be best to let such a creature live; a creature made up mostly from the beasts of the field, but with hands of power, a chin lifting the head upward, and lips holding all things within themselves.

"While he thought upon these things, he took the image in his hands and cast it into the cave.

"But Chemanitou forgot to take out the life!

"The creature lay a long time in the cave and did not stir, for his fall was very great. He lay amongst the old creations that had been thrown in there without life.

"Now when a long time had passed Chemanitou heard a great noise in the cave. He looked in and saw the image sitting there, and he was trying to put together the old broken things that had been cast in as of no value.

"Chemanitou gathered together a vast heap of stones and sand, for large rocks are not to be had upon the island, and stopped up the mouth of the cave. Many days passed and the noise grew louder within the cave. The earth shook, and hot smoke came from the ground. The Manitous crowded to Metowac to see what was the matter.

"Chemanitou came also, for he remembered the image he had cast in there, and forgotten to take away the life.

"Suddenly there was a great rising of the stones and sand; the sky grew black with wind and dust. Fire played about the ground, and water gushed high into the air.

"All the manitous fled with fear; and the image came fourth with a great noise and was most terrible to behold. His life had grown strong within him, for the fire had made it very fierce.

"Everything fled before him and cried; MACHINITO, MACHINITO, which means a god, but an evil god."

The legends of the Indians seem to always take the long way around and add detail that the white mind might perceive as unimportant, and such is the case with this legend relating the origin of evil.

Nonetheless, the imagery is colorful and deserves to be told unabridged.

Chapter Six: Holy Smoke and Sacred Pipes

There is nothing comparable to the feeling you get when sinking your hands into the rich, moist soils of mother earth and extracting an ancient relic. It is much as though she is presenting you with a gift that is both precious and rare. You never know what is hidden just beneath her surface.

It was the autumn of 1990 when I was digging with Kathy at our village site, Old Van Etten Creek. There was a crispness in the air which combined with the fresh pine scent of the woods made me feel invigorated and alive. This particular day mother was very good to me for she gave to me a prehistoric smoking pipe. From the Late Woodland period this pipe is approximately 1,300 years old.

Many people have pierced the flesh of mother earth at this spot I call Old Van Etten Creek, and many have found bits and pieces left behind by the Indians who once lived on these lands. It seems however that she saves special gifts, like the pipe for those who really care. Not far from where my pipe was extracted, but several years apart, my dear friends in archaeology, Bill and Sara Thurman, were

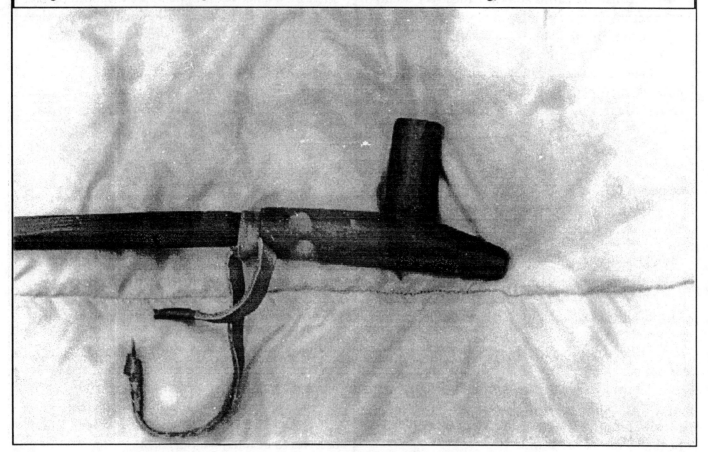

The sacred "peace pipe" or "calumet," an oracle which connects earth and man with heaven and the GreatSpirit. This pipe made of Catlinite is the property of Little Beaver and was made by him.

also given a Late woodland pipe.

These pipes are objects of simplicity upon initial inspection. Your respect grows as you come to learn how they were made, but it quadruples when you learn what the pipe, smoke and tobacco meant spiritually to the Indians.

Even before my recent conversation with Little-Beaver a local medicine man/shaman I was struck by the roundness of the pipe. I wondered of the significance, if any, of this. In telling of the pipe Little-Beaver explained to me about the symbolism connected with the roundness of things in the Native world.

"Everything is round to us, it is not square. Lame Deer said that square is the symbol for white man and this is true. Look, our traditional homes were round. When we dance in private or in pow wow as you saw recently, the dancing was done in circle—round! The motion of the sun and earth is circle and all the planets. Life itself is nothing but circles, a bunch of them linked together. Many believe there are four circles or ages as you would call them. There is much talk today about the year 2,000, the end of things, about your Jesus returning. I believe this is the end of the fourth age of man."

Then Little-Beaver began to explain about the roundness of the pipe, "Look at our pipe for it is awesome, it is spiritual, it is alive and the red stone carries in it our blood."

He continued, "The pipe connects us to the Great Spirit, the wooden stem is that connecting link. White man just plugs some unnatural mixture of tobacco and scents into his pipe bowl and gives it no thought at all. To me all things are represented by the very grains of the tobacco. In the process of using the pipe, the power of the six directions, and all wisdom of all things is represented. To me, to us when that pipe is filled we are at the center of the universe for the pipe becomes the universe!

"You see, through the pipe all this which is our universe is gathered unto us, in your terms it makes us more holy, we become united with the wisdom of the Great Spirit."

Little Beavers words were filled with forcefulness and conviction through which he tried to convey to me of a different background how really important

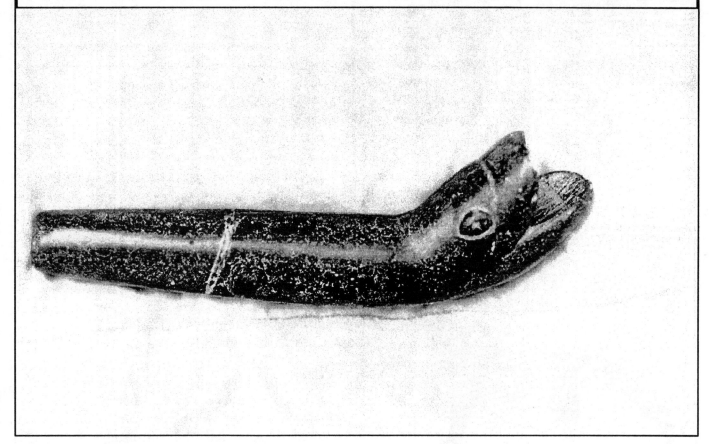

Tobacco pipes come in many effigy forms. This is a prehistoric snake pipe and is carved of a greenstone that is highly polished. This pipe is from the author's collection.

the pipe is. Throughout the religious and social life of the Indian, back into the mists of prehistory, the pipe and the tobacco has been his main companion and friend—to many it remains so today.

Let me tell you a little about how the pipes were made and cared for. To do this lets first return to the pipes Kathy, the Thurman's, and I found.

These pipe were made from clay from the earth at an outcropping not far from the village site. These pipes may have been for social smoking, I feel they had a combined usage. The treatment used in making the pipes though was different than for making pots.

Once the clay was dug from the ground it was loaded into baskets and then transported back to the village. There it was laid out on woven reed mats or tanned hides and it was pulverized. Next all impurities were removed from the clay as any thing that was not supposed to be there could cause problems when the pipe was fired.

Finely crushed rock or shell was then kneaded into the clay, this tempering agent acted to bind the clay and make it stronger after the firing process.

Now the pots of the Late Woodland period all have very rough surfaces. They were nicely made, and around the neck and rim there was a high degree of geometric decoration, but the body of the pot was rough. The pipe however was smoothed very nicely and appears to have had a slip of some sort added to it before firing. Both examples seem to have been highly polished after firing. Bill and Sara's pipe even had a woven cord wrapped around the bowl leaving a decorative impression.

The point is that nothing came easy to these

people of the woods and plains. They took extreme caution in protecting these pipes sometimes even mending them with their own blood.

In his book, *Indians of the Great Lakes,* W. Vernon Kinietz spoke of these bloody repairs. He said, "To render themselves more supple and agile in running and to purge pus from swollen parts, the Hurons made incisions and cuts with small sharp stones into the fat of their legs. With these stones they also drew blood from their arms for the purpose of joining and sticking together broken pieces of their pipes or earthen ware tobacco burning tubes. This is an excellent discovery, and a secret that is much more admirable, as the pieces glued with this blood are afterward stronger than they were before."

The manufacturer of the "medicine pipe" is truly a special act of drawing man and nature together. Depending on which tribe you are speaking of, the pipe stem must be made of a specific wood, generally the wood of the ash tree.

Little-Beaver told that it should be a long straight limb cut to a length of about 20 inches. At one end, using a stone drill or a bone awl, a hole is drilled into the soft pith.

Little-Beaver then revealed the secret of getting a long straight hole all the way through the length of the stick. He explained, "You find yourself a small wood boring grub, they are all around in dead decaying wood, and then you put him into the hole that was started in the stem. Next you cut off a small piece of twig and plug that hole right up.

You hang this over a fire with the plugged end down. The grub wants to escape the heat and so bores his way through the soft pitch to the other end and hollows out the stem. Remember, he has done you a favor and you let him go when his work is done giving him a little thanks for the help."

Little-Beaver's medicine pipe is made of catlinite which he claims to have picked up at a quarry in Minnesota. He speaks proudly of the place and the legends which surround it. He explained that Gitchi Manitou, the Great Spirit, had given to his race the very first medicine pipe. There were great battles fought at the Father of Waters where much Indian blood was spilt, and where this quarry is. Our blood colored those sacred rocks crimson red. It was Gitchi Manitou himself who, being angered at us as

a father would be with squabbling children, commanded that for all time that place should be neutral. After that even tribes that were the most vile of enemies could go to the quarry in safety to take the pipe stone for their medicine pipes."

Little-Beaver's pipe was made in the traditional manner; after the old ways. With a knife of chert the general shape of the pipe was carved into the catlinite. When catlinite is first taken from the ground it is quite soft and easy to work, it remains that way as long as the stone is kept moist. Upon exposure to air the sacred stone becomes very hard.

"I used a pump drill after the ones my forefathers used and I made a straight hole down into the pipe bowl and then another into one end of the bowl until they came together. I sanded down the edges and polished my pipe bowl using water and sand stone."

Next Little Beaver described the process of decorating the pipe stem. This was a matter of great importance also, for not just any decorations could be applied to something so sacred as the medicine pipe.

He explained that, "Some people used porcupine quills that have been dyed colors and they wrap these around the stem near the mouth piece. The porcupine quills placed there represent powerful magic."

In old times, and among those who keep to every detail of sacred tradition, the tobacco for the medicine pipe needed to be cut on a special board. Great care needed to be taken so as to not offend the Great Spirit, for if even a grain fell upon mother earth he might mistakenly feel she had been given the first offering.

Gray Wolf in his book, *The Indians Secret World,* spoke of those things which must be done before even filling the pipe bowl. He said, "A small pinch should be held up as an offering to the Great Spirit. The next pinch must be held down as an offering to Mother Earth. Then offerings would be extended to north, south, east and west, always starting with the east, for from the east comes light and wisdom. With each offering a prayer would be said.

"The pipe must be lit by placing a coal from the fire on top of the tobacco rather than by using a burning twig, which would tend to blacken the bowl."

Now the pipe was used in many, many ceremonies and there were specific rules to follow. For example in sacred council the ritual of filling the pipe as described by Gray Wolf must be adhered to. It was then always passed to the person on your left and traveling in the direction of the sun. The stem must always be pointing toward the teepee wall as in a lodge ceremony the teepee represents the universe and outside the lodge the world itself represents Gitchi Manitou who is every where.

The pipe can never ever pass the door. When it reaches the individual closest to the entrance the pipe is passed back around the circle unsmoked until it reaches the person seated nearest the door.

Great and mystical prayers are offered up during this time, prayers contained within the living pipe, in passing the door the prayers might escape. After the smoking has been completed then the pipe is stood against a brace and the stem is pointed toward the heavens with the bowl resting on the ground. In this way, the pipe is again a connecting link between heaven and earth.

"It is important," Little-Beaver told me, "to remember always that to smoke the pipe is to pray for in a very real way it is your altar."

In *Mystic Warriors of the Plains,* Thomas E. Mails aptly described how the pipe symbolized oneness. He said, "As he filled the pipe, the leader called upon the Great Spirit to behold it, adding that the smoke from his tobacco would cover everything upon the earth, and even reach to the heavens. He would then ask that the nation's people would be as the smoke. The pipe smoke was the bearer of a heaven sent voice, and all the wildlife and the six directions joined in the smokers sending it. This showed that the Indians were thinking of the soul and of death, and was a sure sign they were humiliating themselves before the Great Spirit, since they knew they were as dust before him who was everything and all powerful."

Tobacco was heavily cultivated by the Late Woodland tribes of the north east, and on a lesser degree by the Indians of the plains. It is interesting to note what this sacred mixture was composed of. The tobacco was mixed with many other things such as sumac, the dried bark from the red alder, red willow and dogwood. This special blend was called kinnikinnick. Remarkably, and perhaps attesting to its spiritual holiness, this mixture has none of the harmful effect of the smoke currently consumed by a cancer infested public.

The peace pipe or calumet seems as though it had a universal adaptation to the Indian tribes throughout north America. The calumet may have seen its most noble usage in the northeast where a ceremony called the "calumet dance" was performed.

The purpose of the calumet dance was to strengthen in peace time and for uniting in war time, it was also for public rejoicing as well as to ensure a prosperous voyage.

This ceremony was also known as the Spirit Dance. The dancing was done to honor the calumet. Words used in the songs interconnected with the dance were invocations to the spirit world. It is also known that this dance was used to call the souls of those who battle was to be waged against thus making certain that combat would be successful.

Perhaps the earliest account of the dance was written by Allouez in 1667 as he observed the dance among the Miami Indians. He wrote, "They acknowledge many spirits to whom they offer sacrifice. They practice a kind of dance, which they call the dance of the tobacco pipe. It is executed thus: they prepare a great pipe, which they deck with plumes, and put in the middle of the room with a sort of veneration. One of the company rises, begins to dance, and then yields his place to another, and this one to a third; and thus they dance in succession, one after another and not together. One would take this dance for a pantomime ballet; and it is executed to the beating of a drum. The performer makes war in rhythmic time, preparing his arms, attiring himself, running, discovering the foe, raising the cry, slaying the enemy, removing his scalp, and returning home with a cry of victory, and all with astonishing exactness, promptitude and agility. After they have all danced, one after the other, around the pipe, it is taken and offered to the chief man in the whole assembly, for him to smoke; then to another, and so in succession to all. This ceremony resembles in its significance the French custom of drinking, several out of the same glass; but in addition, the pipe is left in the keeping of the most honored man, as a sacred trust, and a sure pledge of the peace and union that will ever subsist among them as long as they shall remain in that person's hands."

Of the calumet pipe itself, a wonderful description was written in 1670 by Perrot of its use among the Mascoutens. Perrot wrote; "The old man held in his hand a calumet of red stone, with a long stick at the end; this was ornamented in its whole length with the heads of birds that were flame colored, and had in the middle a bunch of feathers colored bright red which resembled a great fan. As soon as he espied the leader of the Frenchmen, he presented to him the calumet, on the side next to the sun; and uttered words which were apparently addressed to all the spirits whom those people adore. The old man held it sometimes toward the east, and sometimes toward the west; then toward the sun; now he would stick the end in the ground, and then he would turn the calumet around him looking at it as if he were trying to point out the whole earth, with expressions which gave the Frenchman to understand that he had compassion on all men. Then he rubbed with his hand Perrot's head, back, legs and feet, and sometimes his own body. This welcome lasted a long time, during which the old man made a harangue, after the fashion of a prayer, all to assure the Frenchman of the joy which all in the village felt at his arrival."

The pipe came into play in almost every aspect of the Indian life. Its importance cannot be overstated. I am sure I repeat myself when I remind that the pipe was the communicator between god and man and that the smoke carries prayers from earth heavenward.

The Ottawa Indians used the pipe in a ceremony to insure good hunting. At a particular point in this ceremony the man appointed to take care of the tobacco breaks it in two, and throws it into the fire. Everyone cries out loud while the tobacco burns and the smoke rises aloft.

It found use among the plains tribes as a sort of spiritual lie detector.

If an Indian told a story that sounded somewhat far fetched then the shaman would prepare the pipe to see if the truth was being told. The pipe stem was painted red and the pipe was prayed over. It was asked of the Great Spirit that if the man was lying that his days would be short in number, but if the truth was being told then his life might be quite long.

The spiritual discerner was then passed to the man who was invited to smoke from it, however he was warned by the shaman. He knew that his story had to be sure as the bowl of the pipe, and as straight as the hole through the stem which was bored by the little grub, or that his days were in danger of being numbered. If the pipe was refused the person was generally looked upon as having not spoken the truth.

Medicine pipes that were kept in sacred bundles were considered to have potent powers for healing and bringing good fortune to the people. The supernatural powers of these pipes could only be put into service by their owners, and then only during very solemn ceremony. Then the medicine pipe was wrapped in a bundle which contained other items necessary for pipe ceremonies. These bundles included such items as rattles and paint. The bundle itself was made of fur. These bundles were hung on the teepee pole above the owners head.

The calumet attained, as stated, its highest degree of ceremonial usage in the north east, however, the Blackfoot Indians of the plains adapted the use of the calumet or medicine pipe. There the pipe evolved into quite a different form called the, "Thunder Pipe." This owing to the fact that the Blackfoot thought the pipes were a divine gift to them from the thunder.

These ceremonial pipes were very long, as much as thirty to sixty inches in length! Remember the average medicine pipe was about twenty to twenty five inches long.

The pipe as used by the Blackfoot had red and green stripes and a clump of black hair around the middle. Incredibly the pipe was also inset with human teeth.

One such pipe was reported as being covered with an entire eagle, with the eagle considered very powerful it is not difficult to understand its use in conjunction with the powerful pipe.

In his book, *Mystic Warriors of the Plains,* Thomas Mails commented on the Blackfoot tradition. He said, "The numerous appurtenant pieces in known Blackfoot pipe bundles included the fetus of a deer; squirrel, muskrat, mink, and bird skins; necklaces; and many other objects. The owner was expected to open the bundle at the first thunder in the spring and when someone had vowed to make the Sun Dance with the pipe stem. It was also opened when a bundle was to be transferred to a purchaser. Its special benefit was to its owner, giving him wisdom, status, and protection. He was, however, obliged to submit to many fanciful and demanding rules. Examples are that he was only allowed to point with his thumb and could not pick up any object that he found; he had to hold his pipe in a particular way; he must never sit on his bedding. His wife had to make smudge every morning and shift the position of the bundle in fixed sunwise sequence, and under no condition was it to touch the ground. These seem to be unnecessary cautions, yet they kept the owners mind continually on the bundle and its purpose."

In the north east one such "unusual" custom applied to the smoking of the medicine pipe was that a man whose wife was pregnant had to abstain from smoking the pipe in council. It was believed that if he did not do this his wife would not be safely delivered of her child and that the latter would inevitably die.

Many archeologists today hold the Indian of prehistory and early contact period in very low esteem. They view him as a pathetic creature who was poor of nature and completely dependent on the whims of his environment. He is pictured as having to scavenge for food and to have never attained a high degree of civilization, who even at his cultural pinnacle was still in a barbaric state. Looking at the religious customs and the reverence with which they were carried out I find this a terrible miscalculation.

Francis du Peron penned a letter to his brother in 1639 which gave a less than glowing account of the Huron Indians of the north east. But notice that even in this description, as lowly and destitute as it paints him, the ever present pipe.

"Their only covering is a beaver skin which they wear upon their shoulders in the form of a mantle; shoes and leggings in the winter, a tobacco pouch behind the back, a pipe in the hand; around their necks and arms bead necklaces and bracelets of porcelain; they also suspended these from their ears, and around their locks of hair. They grease their hair and their faces; they also streak their faces with black and red paint."

In dire times, and there were those as there is with any culture, the pipe was their main social solace. Henry R. Schoolcraft in his 1851, *History of the Indians,* said of this, "Let it not be supposed however that the Indians life while on wintering grounds is a round feasting. Quite the contrary; and his feasts are often followed by long and painful fasts. Under all sufferings, the pipe of the hunter is his chief solace, and is the solace often resorted to. Smoking parties are frequently formed when there is a scarcity of food not tending, as might be supposed, to destroy social feelings and render the temper sour. On these occasions the entertainer sends a message to this effect; Come smoke with me. I have no food, but we can pass away the evening very well without it."

For me the pipe became very special one day while sitting and talking with Chief John Nahgog-won. He told me that he had been digging in his backyard and had uncovered two clay pipe bowls. He got them out to show me. They were trade pipes, the type used throughout the 1700 and 1800's to buy furs and other commodities from the Indians. You could tell that John really loved those pipes.

With a large, kind smile playing across his face Chief Nahgogwon handed one of the pipes to me and said, "Here, I want you to have this." To me, knowing the background of his people and the sacredness of the pipe, I considered this a true act of genuine friendship between the Chief and I.

Masked mountain spirits dance to keep evil entities away.

Chapter Seven: Special Places Where the Spirits and Souls Dwell

Commins, Michigan is a small rural community. The people there are of strong Amish descent. It is a friendly place, a good place to visit, probably a good place to live. Every fall there is held at Commins, "Indian Days." At this time Indians gather from all over the state and bring their crafts to sell. The Indians give demonstrations of the Native American way of life. Everyone who attends has a very good time.

In the fall of 1988 Kathy and I attended the festivities and had arranged before hand to do a video interview with Eli Thomas, Chief Little Elk. He was in his mid eighties but sharp as a tack. The interview was wonderful, we conducted it in a teepee. He reminisced about his childhood, and he sang songs in the Indian tongue that his mother had sung to him as a child.

Then something very special happened. Kathy, myself and two others were invited to escort Little Elk to a special fresh water springs where he would bless the spirit of the springs in the tradition which his people have followed for longer than anyone can remember.

I had never heard of the springs so the Chief explained, "In dhat boilin' spring, daht water jess comes up out of da Mother Earth. When I'm travelin' I gotta stop by dhere. Dhere's a spirit in dhere. A person gotta leavve some tobacco dhere, maybe a little bit of what you eat. Now you gotta do daht, dhats da way da old timers done it. Dhat's what we gotta do."

So the five of us drove to the springs. Well actually you drive within a mile of it and then walk in. Chief Little Elk lead the way. Just before we got to the springs we each took a turn at sprinkling tobacco to the four directions in paying homage to Mother Earth. Then we approached the springs.

This spring is the source of a creek. It is a shallow pool where the ice cold water boils up stirring the clean white sand in abstract visions of yesterdays and tomorrows. The action looks very much like a

51

hand or breath is just below the surface fanning the sands and water into action.

This was a sacred place, a place where a spirit dwelled beneath the waters and you could feel a presence. The Chief offered some prayers in the native tongue which I did not understand, and then we sprinkled more tobacco. With that it was over, but I had felt honored to be included in such a solemn and time honored tradition. Also this was the first time that I had been to such a "holy place" of nature.

Mysterious sounds and physical aberrations are not uncommon today in association with specific manitou dwelling places or points of worship. It seems that many of these places have not lost their potency over the centuries.

One such place exists near the United States/Canada border near Sault Ste. Marie, Michigan. On a high precipice there stood a manitou tree which has long since vanished. Unusual phenomenon is still reported near where the tree is thought to have stood. Nausea, light headedness are frequently reported from visitors to this site.

The account of the tree was originally recorded by Henry R. Schoolcraft in the mid 1800's. Schoolcraft told, "There is a prominent hill in the vicinity of Sault Ste. Marie at the outlet of Lake Superior. An Indian foot path formerly connected this hill with the old French settlement at those falls, from which it is distant about a mile. In the intermediate space, near the path, there formerly stood a tree, a large mountain ash, from which, Indian tradition says, there issued a sound, resembling that produced by their own war drums, during the most calm and cloudless days. This occurred long before the French appeared in the country. It was consequently regarded as the local residence of a spirit, and deemed sacred."

This is strongly reminiscent of the mysterious sounds of thunder emanating from Thunder Bay near Alpena—we discussed this earlier. The Schoolcraft account describes the manner of offerings given, as well as the demise of the tree. It is interesting to note that the offerings were of twigs and boughs. Both of these items are significant in the shaking-tent rite as the floor of the tent is lined with them.

Schoolcraft continued, "From that time they began to deposit at its foot, an offering of small green twigs and boughs, whenever they passed the path, so that in process of time, a high pile of these offerings of the forest was accumulated. It seemed as if, by this procedure, the other trees had each made an offering to this tree. At length the tree blew down, during a violent storm, and has since entirely decayed, but the spot was recollected and the offerings kept up, and they would have continued to the present hour had not an accidental circumstance put a stop to it.

"In the month of July 1822, the government sent a military force to take post at the Sault, and one of the first acts of the commanding officer was to order out a fatigue party to cut a wagon road from the selected site of the post to the hill. This road was directed to be cut sixty feet wide, and it passed over the site of the tree. The pile of offerings was thus removed, without the men knowing that it had ever had a spiritual origin; and thus the practice itself came to an end."

Schoolcraft pointed out that the Indians were prone to the instruction of their prophets in believing that the coming of white man fulfilled predictions of the arrival of white "harbingers of evil." Certainly desecrating such sacred grounds does nothing to relieve this thought. It goes without saying that the prophets were right, that the white destroyed the race as it existed and have subsequently ruined the environment through lack of respect and common sense. The Indian culture, left alone to develop would have become a powerful force in this world, undoubtedly with substantial

efforts to preserve the lands and waters which gave them life rather than degrading their sacredness!

Special places where the spirits dwell, be they of human or other, seem to often be grave sites. It is no great secret that the mounds of prehistory were such places. The most elaborate of grave goods were made and placed with the dead so that these items could accompany them into the "paradise" which follows this life. Although archaeology does not record the intangible, I imagine that a shaman presided over the creation of such ceremonial objects.

In many cases after these artistic creations were completed the shaman did something unthinkable to the white mind. He would kill the item by breaking it! The killing released the spirit of the relic to enter into the paradise world with the soul of the deceased. In some tribal cultures there was also the practice of leaving a hole in the grave so that the spirit could escape.

Wonderful earth mounds of spiritual significance are to be found from Ohio on down through the more southern states. Of particular interest is the Great Serpent Mound in Ohio. There is record of a mound at Grave Creek Flats, Virginia which shows the complexity of the burial practices which the shaman's of ancient times presided over.

Schoolcraft recorded that there were a series of mounds at the junction of Big and Little Grave Creeks with the Ohio River. One in particular held his interest due at first to its very large size. He also noticed that all these mounds were connected by

low earthen entrenchments which were, at the time of his visit it 1843, still quite visible. This mound group also had a stone well which sounds very much like the one described earlier as from the Black River Stone Works.

The largest mound was said to be conical with the top cut off. At the highest point this mound is said to have been 50 feet tall! Schoolcraft said, "This area is quite level and commands a view of the entire area, and of the river above and below, and the west shores of the Ohio in front. Any public transaction on this area would be visible to the multitudes all around it, and it has in this respect all the advantages of the Mexican and Yucatanese tecalli."

That Schoolcraft, a well traveled man who had seen many sites of prehistoric America, should compare this in design to the structures of the Yucatan in Mexico is interesting. These were the great ceremonial centers where shamanism reached its highest degree of perfection in the ancient world.

Something unusual has occurred with these mounds of the woodlands and the south east. Often times stones inscribed with alphabets from other portions of the world have turned up. Professional archaeology has in modern times tried to debunk them rather than rewrite the history books, but they were accepted by the forefathers of modern archaeology.

Schoolcraft described just such an unusual stone as having come from the mounds at Grave Creek Flats. He explained, "The most interesting object of antiquarian inquiry is a small flat stone inscribed with antique alphabetic characters, which was disclosed on the excavation of the large mound. These characters are in the ancient Celtic tradition of sixteen right and acute angled single strokes, and which is parent of modern Runic as well as the Bardic."

One cannot discount that ancient European cultures visited the shores inhabited by the American Indians and that either their practices influenced the shamanistic rites of the Indians, or the other way around. We will discuss some other alphabetically inscribed stones latter in this chapter, but for now lets return to the mound.

In 1843 Mr. Schoolcraft penned an atmospheric description of this mound. As you read it imagine, if you will, the great ceremony which must have surrounding every aspect of its creation.

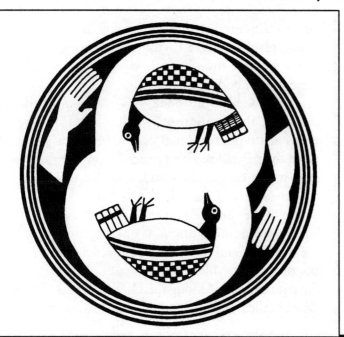

"The great mound at these flats was opened as a place of public resort about four years ago. For this purpose a horizontal gallery to its center was dug and bricked up, and provided with a door. The center of the mound was a rotunda of about twenty five feet diameter, and a shaft sunk from the top to intersect it; it was in these excavations that the skeletons and accompanying relics and ornaments were found. All these articles are arranged in the rotunda for exhibition. The chamber is lit by candles. The lowermost skeleton is almost entire, and in a good state of preservation and is put up by wires on the walls. It measures over six feet tall! The skeletons in the upper vault where the stone was found are nearly all destroyed.

"It is a damp and gloomy repository, and exhibits in the roof and walls of the rotunda one of the most extraordinary sepulchral displays which the world affords. On casting the eye up to the ceiling, and the heads of the pillars supporting it, it is found to be encrusted with, or rather festooned with a white, soft, flaky mass of matter, which had exuded from the mound above. This apparently animal exudation is as white as snow. It hangs in pendant masses and globular drops; the surface is covered with large globules of clear water, which in the reflected light have all the brilliancy of diamonds. These drops of water trickle to the door, and occasionally the exuded white matter falls. The wooden pillars are furnished with the appearance of capitals, by this substance. That it is highly charged with particles of matter, rising from the decay or incineration of human bodies, is the only theory by which we might account for this phenomenon. Curious and antique it certainly is, and with the faint light of a few candles it would not require much imagination to invest the entire rotunda with sylphlike forms of the sheeted dead."

The description of the white matter is curiously like that of ectoplasm from spiritual ceremonies, not to mention a similarity to the angel hair enigma associated with the appearance of UFO's. Also latter, a second alphabetically inscribed stone was found in one of the smaller mounds.

To the north, in Newark, Ohio is found the Octagon Mound group. This is an exciting religious center which speaks very much of a commingling of ancient religious and shamanistic traditions in ancient America.

When I speak of these particular mounds and earthworks and I say small, even these are large. The Newark Mounds cover a large area and many have been destroyed by civilization. From the air they present an unusual geometric pattern, but seem to represent nothing really significant at first glance.

Dr. Arnold Murry looked at these mounds and entrenchments from the air and with his expertise discovered that this mound system tells the story of the life cycle on a grand scale!

A large circle depicts the womb where life is nurtured, and there is an opening, the cervix which opens into the birthing canal, which in turn leads to another large circle—the circle of life. Emanating from this circle are side roads representing paths taken in life, but always return to the circle. Now off the birth canal is another path, the "Path of Souls," which leads to the Great Octagon Mound, thought to represent "Paradise."

In two of these mounds were found stone that were highly shaped and which were inscribed with ancient Hebrew! One stone has not yet been translated, but the more ornate of the two has on it the ten commandments of Moses!

If Dr. Murray is correct in his interpretation of this site then perhaps the next place we should look at is Paradise, for to the Indians, indeed to most cultures of the world, it is as real as any place that we can feel or touch.

Without exception all American Indians place their Paradise to the west. Not indicating that the Great Plains are Paradise, as even the Indians of the Plains place Paradise to the west. No, it is some where beyond the physical west that we know in these mortal bodies.

J.G. Kohl in his book, *Kitchi-Gamill,* tried to pin point the location of paradise based on interviews with Native Americans. He states, "They place their Paradise far beyond the prairism as they say—at the end of the world, and that their imagination seeks and finds it in following the brilliant course of the sun and planets. I fancy the whole idea has an astronomical origin, if I may be permitted to use the term, and this view is supported by the Indians calling the Milky Way the path of the dead, or the path of souls. Among the Ojibbeways, the Milky Way is called Jibekana, which word has that meaning. They would scarcely place their path of souls so high if they merely wished their dead to reach the prairies, or if they did not rather wish them to hurry after the setting sun." Of the Path of Souls which leads to Paradise, I have learned that it is a straight path with side roads. There is a great strawberry that lay in the path, a river which must be crossed, and a great snake which lay before the entrance.

It is said that the Great Spirit has planted his law on earth and that like a tree it grows straight upwards. There is a strong similarity here with the Miday symbolic use of the "tree of life." Many get onto the side paths, but when a man dies they all go down the path of souls.

It seems to me that entrance into Paradise does not depend on how good or bad you might have been during life, but rather on what you can over come on your journey down the path of the souls.

For example the Indians of the eastern woodland believe that laying next to this path is a great strawberry which looks sweet, luscious and tempting. A dark man, cloaked in shadows stands by this object of desire and invites all who pass by to partake of it. To fall into temptation and eat of this fruit is to have your soul lost for all time to come. Where this lost soul goes though is somewhat confusing for I can find no concept of a hell like place in the eastern mythology.

For those who overcome the temptation their journey towards Paradise continues without obstruction, that is until they are almost there. This sojourn of the soul is said to require three to four days.

As Paradise comes into sight there also comes one last obstacle, this in the form of a mysterious river. This river has no bridge, and some tribes say it is not a river at all, but rather a large twisting serpent or snake.

An unnamed Indian elder explained further in the book, *KitchiGami*. He said, "Over the river is something which looks like a great tree stump laying across it. Its roots are firmly fastened on the opposite shore. On this side it raises its head, but it does not quite reach to the land. There is a small gap over which souls must hop. The log to is constantly shaking. Most of the souls spring across, balance themselves properly, and save themselves. Those, however, that jump short, or slip off the bridge, fall into the water, and are converted to toads or fishes.

Hence it is not good when the deceased are bound to a board, for otherwise they might move freely, and, perchance, save themselves by swimming. If fastened to a board, they can easily be carried down with the stream. Little children, too, fare very badly here, because they are not good jumpers, and so they perish in great numbers at the bridge. Hence our mothers can never be consoled when their children die before the time when. they could help themselves along the road to paradise."

Paradise is a place that was not originally conceived by the Great Spirit. It was his wish that man would be happy and contented on earth. But the evil spirit, who we took a look at earlier, brought wickedness, sickness, death and all manner of ills upon men. Manabozho, the spiritual guardian of man was called upon by the Great Spirit to create Paradise for man in the far west. Manabozho is said to have created a very beautiful place—a spiritual reflection of earth. Monabozho himself is also said to greet those who arrive successfully.

In the Bible of Christianity, Cherubs with flaming swords stood at the entrance of Eden barring Adam and Eve from reentering after their fall. In the north American Indian mysticism souls are barred from leaving Paradise. An enormous dog is said to lie across the path. He allows everyone traveling to the west to make their trip without interference. No one is allowed to travel eastward back to the land of the living.

But there are those who somehow appeased the dog and did indeed return to the land of the living to tell of what the after life, the eternal state, is like.

One of the finest accounts was preserved, again by Henry R. Schoolcraft. His 1851 book, *History of the Indians,* is filled with rare items far surpassing gem stones in their delightful reflective quality. These gems, however, give us a very true insight into American Indian life and tradition.

In a story called, "The White Stone Canoe," we find the account of a young brave's journey to Paradise. The story tells, "There was once a very beautiful young girl, who died suddenly on the day she was to have been married to a handsome young man. He was also brave, but his heart was not proof against this loss. From the hour she was buried, there was no more joy or peace for him. He went often to visit the spot where the women had buried her, and sat musing there, when, it was thought by some of his friends, he would have done better to try to amuse himself in the chase, or by diverting his thoughts in the war-path. But war and hunting had both lost their charms for him. His heart was already dead within him. He pushed aside both his war-club and his bow and arrow."

Now this young man was determined to find the "path of souls," and find the soul of his lost love. I wonder why the concept of suicide had not occurred to him, but honorably he was to find a different way down that path.

To continue with the Schoolcraft account, "At length he spied a path. It lead him through a grove, then up a long and elevated ridge, on the very top of which he came to a lodge. At the door stood an old man, with white hair, whose eyes, though deeply sunk, had a fiery brilliancy. He had a long robe of skins thrown loosely around his shoulders, and a staff in his hands. It was Chebiabos.

"The young Chippewa began to tell his story; but the venerable chief arrested him, before he proceeded to speak ten words. "I have expected you," he replied, "and had just risen to bid you welcome to my abode. She whom you seek passed here but a few days since, and being fatigued with her journey, rested herself here. Enter my lodge and be seated, and then I will satisfy your inquiries and give you directions for your journey from this point." Having done this they both issued forth to the lodge door. "You see yonder gulf," he said, "and the wide stretching blue plains beyond. It is the land of souls. You stand upon its borders, and my lodge is the gate of entrance. But you cannot take your body along. Leave it here with your bow and arrows, your bundle and your dog. You will find them safe of your return."

In this account there is quite a discrepancy as to what the entrance to Paradise is like.

"So saying, he re-entered the lodge, and the freed traveler bounded forward, as if his feet had suddenly been endowed with the power of wings. All things retained their natural color and shape. The woods and leaves, and streams and lakes, were only more bright and comely than he had ever witnessed. Animals bounded across his path, with a freedom and confidence which seemed to tell him, there was no blood shed here. Birds of beautiful plumage inhabited the grooves, and sported in the waters. There was but one thing in which he saw a very unusual effect. He noticed that his passage was not stopped by trees or other objects. He appeared to walk directly through them. They were, in fact but the souls of the material trees. He became sensible that he was in the land of shadows. When he had traveled half a days journey, through a country which was continually becoming more attractive, he came to the banks of a broad lake, in the center of which was a large and beautiful island. He found a canoe of shinning white stone tied to the shore. He was now sure that he had come the right path, for the aged man had told him of this. There were also shinning paddles. He immediately entered the canoe, and took the paddles in his hands, when to his joy and surprise, on turning around, he beheld the object of his search in another canoe, exactly its counter part in everything. She had exactly imitated his motions, and they were side by side. They at once pushed out from shore and began to cross the lake. Its waves seemed to be rising, and at a distance looked ready to swallow them up; but just as they entered the whitened edge of them they seemed to melt away, as if they were but images of waves. But no sooner was one wreath of foam passed, and another, more threatening still rose up. Thus they were in perpetual fear; and what added to it, was the clearness of the water, through which they could see heaps of beings who had perished before, and whose bones lay strewed on the bottom of the lake. The Master of Life had, however, decreed to let them pass, for the actions of neither of them had been bad. But they saw many others struggling and sinking in the waves. Old men and young men, males and females of all ages and ranks were there; some passed, and some sank. It was only the little children whose canoes seemed to meet no waves. At length, every difficulty was gone, as in a moment, and they both leaped out on the happy island. They felt that the very air was food. It strengthened and nourished them. They wandered together over the blissful fields, where everything was formed to please the eye and the ear. There were no tempests there was no ice, no chilly winds, no one shivered for the want of warm clothes: no one suffered for hunger, no one mourned the dead. They saw no graves. They heard of no wars. There was no hunting of animals; for the air itself was their food. Gladly would the young warrior have remained forever, but he was obliged to go back for his body. He did not see the Master of Life, but he heard his voice in the soft breeze. "Go back," said this voice, "to the land from whence you come. Your time has not yet come. The duties for which I made you, and which you are to perform are not yet finished. Return to your people and accomplish the duties of a good man. You will be the ruler of your tribe for many days. The rules you must observe will be told you by messenger who keeps the gate. When he surrenders back your body, he will tell you what to do. Listen to him, and you shall afterwards rejoin the spirit which you must now leave behind. She is accepted, and will ever be here, as young and as happy as she was when I first called her from the land of snows."

Accounts of the place called "Paradise" and the "Path of Souls" which leads there vary considerably from tribe to tribe. In *Kitchi Gami* another account is given which is also important to look at as it gives more insight to the Indian Paradise.

"The hunter was sick- very sick. He was drawing neigh his end. He seemed to be dead, and his soul went on the great wandering. He marched straight to the west towards the setting sun. At first he had to make his way through an extraordinary quantity of forest, scrub, and wilderness. There was no path there. At length he found a trail and narrow paths. These little paths came from every quarter. There were very many of them, the paths of all the dead souls from all the tribes and villages of the Indians, which at length formed into one great broad trail. Then he began to march along rapidly. Shortly before, his cousin and friend had died, and he hoped to catch him up. He knew that his cousin had taken with him neither a gun nor a cooking kettle. He himself, however, had two guns and two kettles with him, and would gladly divide them with his cousin. Hence he hurried on.

"At length he arrived at the great strawberry. Near it stood a person, wrapped up in the black plumage of a raven. The raven spoke to him:

" 'Whither art thou going?'

" 'He replied; To the end of my path.'

" 'Thou art tired, stay a little while.'

" 'I will not.'

" 'Thou art hungry. Taste this. Take it.'

"He went straight through. Without finding his cousin, he reached the great river that surrounds Paradise. He wandered for a long time along the bank, and could not find the bridge. At last he heard a cry.

"He followed the call, and found that it was not a person as he fancied, who shouted so, but the great log, which lay its anchor on its roots, and in its moving up and down produced such a creaking sound, just like the old trees in the forest, when the wind rattles them and they rub against other trees, are wont to utter. He succeeded in crossing, and entered the land of the souls. It was a remarkably large village. Longways and broadways, as far as the eye could see, huts and tents were erected closely together on the meadows and along the river. The end of the village could not be seen. A long distance off the murmur of the songs and the noise of the countless drums that were beaten could be heard. On all sides were sports and amusements going on. On the meadows they were playing the jeu a la crosse.

"The hunter sought his deceased parents in the throng, and though he at first fancied he should be unable to find them, they soon joined him. The mother was highly delighted, but the father was serious, frowned and asked; Why are you here my son?

"He tried to send him back at once, but the mother prevented it, and held her son tightly, and led him to her wigwam. She told him that he was very sick looking, but that he wasn't dead yet. She invited him to come in and refresh himself and to eat. She gave him something that looked like dried meat but it glistened like fungus, and he did not like it.

"The father again asked what he was doing there and reminded him that he had children still at home. And so at last he was obliged to go. The mother took a very sorrowful parting from him, and wrapped in paper something that looked like vermillion powder, put it in a box, and gave it to him, saying, 'That will do thee good.'

"The return was accompanied by much greater terrors. When he came to the river, he found its waters foaming and dashing as if in a storm. The banks were covered with many fragments of wood. These were the remains of many shipwrecked and broken children's cradles, which he had noticed on his arrival. He noticed a hissing and rattling as if of serpents, and that the log had converted into a mighty serpent. It writhed and crested so that he began to feel rather frightened; still, he must go across, as his father said, and return to his little ones. Hence, he sprang forward, and reached the opposite bank with great difficulty and trouble.

"When he arrived at the strawberry, that was also changed. What seemed to him before a pink strawberry was now a red hot mass. By its side no longer stood a friendly inviting bird, but a great savage man who swung a heavy hammer in his hand, and menaced him. Still, the hunter would not allow himself to be frightened, and went on undisturbed.

"After some time he found his cousin on the road, who must have marched very slowly, and whom he had passed before, in his zeal, without noticing. He tried at first to persuade him to turn back with him, but his cousin would not. He was really dead, and must go to the land of souls. So he gave him one of his kettles and his guns, and some good advice in the bargain, and let him go on.

"At last he lost his way. So long as the path was broad, it was all right; but when the little side paths began to branch off, he could no longer find the trail of his village. He lost his way in the prairie, and suddenly found himself encompassed by smoke and flames, for the prairies were burning all around. At first he was afraid he should never see his children again, but he cast himself into the sea of flames. Terror, however, agitated him so greatly, that he drew a deep breath and awoke.

"When he had opened his eyes a little, he heard sobbing and weeping around him. It was his children and wife, who were standing round his bed, and mourning him as one dead.

" 'I have been in the land of souls. I have seen my mother, but have returned to you, he said, to console them: and then straightway remembering the charm his mother gave him, he begged his wife to feel if there were not something in his bag: he was to weak to do it himself. The squaw produced a small birch bark box, and in it she found a piece of paper, in which was wrapped a pretty little blood sponge. He kept this receipt by him, ate some of it, and then lived for a long time with his squaw and children."

Thus are a few of the places where the spirits and souls dwell. There are of course many more, but these will have to wait for another time.

Chapter Eight: Dreams, Visions and Prophets of The Great Spirit

I can not help but marvel at how North American Indian culture is so diverse from tribe to tribe—even within a close area. There are, however, certain things which show little variation from group to group. The extreme significance of pipe smoking is one which we have already examined. Another area which ties deeply into the spiritual beliefs of the Indian is dreams, visions.

One need only look at the vision quest practiced among almost all American Indians. A plethora of material has been entered into American literature on this subject so we will touch only briefly upon it later in this chapter.

Dreams, however, have been a mystical influ-

ence on all cultures of the world. They have influenced great wars and great discoveries. Dreams are the stuff of which prophecy is made of. Look at St. John on the island of Patmos.

To me, dreams held little significance, that is until I became interested in the Indian culture. I told you earlier about the "image stone" I found in my backyard. I purposely left out for this chapter the influence dreams had on particular episode.

I related to you that my dog Samson had uncovered pottery in our backyard and that my wife Kathy and I excavated about 1200 pieces of pottery and other associated relics. What I did not tell you is that for months before the actual events, I had dreams nearly every night of relics being found in our backyard at that particular spot! There was another such spot under a large oak tree, though excavations could not be done there due to the root system and our signed agreement to sell the house. I will always wonder what lay beneath the sands in my former yard.

But who among the Indians dreams the dreams or who has the visions? Well of course they all do. But does anyone's dream have more import than others? Well, naturally those of the shaman or powerful chief held the heaviest weight.

There were also the Winkles, special prophets whose dreams held great significance. Who or what were the Winkles? Well, they were men who dressed like women. They did this by their own choice through instruction received via dreams. According to John Lame Deer the Great Spirit made them this way and endowed on them the gift of prophecy. It is also told that a father would give a horse to have one of these "she-men" name his child, as there was believed to be very powerful medicine in a name chosen by the Winkles.

The Winkles prophets are said to have a very special origin.

They begin as twins of different sexes growing

60

in the womb and through some spiritual manifestation they are merged into one. Though they were considered sacred, the father of young boys did not like them to be around the Winkles and instructed them to keep their distance.

In times now long past the Winkles used to refer to each other as sisters. They were not buried with others but rather together on a special hill.

Naturally the dreams of the shaman are extremely powerful. It is interesting to point out here that a shaman learns his path in life through a dream—in particular, the vision quest. It is at that time that the young man who has reached puberty learns whether he will be a hunter, shaman or warrior.

Dreams, dances and medicine go hand in hand. If during the course of an illness a dance is deemed necessary it is so ordered by the shaman.

Dreams are believed to be the language of the soul. For those who consider astral projection to be of eastern origin I say look again. The souls separation from the body during the dream state was and is still very much employed by the Indians.

I met an elderly Indian lady at the Mikado, Michigan Reservation. Her name escapes me now, but she looked ancient, as though she had always been here to watch the slow parade of time. She told me that when she sleeps her soul often leaves her body and wanders to any place it so desires. She also claims that during these ethereal wanderings that she can steal the souls of others. I wondered about

her, but dared not ask if she was a Mock-wa-mosa, the Bear Walker.

Such beliefs though were part of the record from the early contact period. Christian missionaries found that the Huron Indians believed that their souls detached from their bodies during sleep, and wandered completely independent of the body's control.

Again early missionaries to the northeast were astounded by the strong faith given to dreams. The Huron's considered them as direct orders from Gitchi-manitou, the Great Spirit. Without delay orders received in dreams had to be carried out. It was also found that in order for an individual's dreams to be carried out without question that he had to be a person of higher than average standing in his group and that dreams of his had in the past come true. It was delegated to the parent to dream for the child. And if the dream was of a symbolic nature it was left to the shaman to interpret and act upon.

Most Indian men went to lonely secluded places to obtain their visions. At such places it was not uncommon for spirits to come to the individual to aid him. To assist in the desired vision coming with more swiftness, the Crow Indian would practice self sacrifice, sometimes cutting off a small piece of the finger.

There are those people who cannot for some reason have a vision of their own. To these people provision is made. They can buy a vision and medicine bundle from a shaman. Though these sacred accouterments were seldom as powerful as those obtained by the seeker himself.

The special vision which affected the course of the entire life was generally obtained at an early age, usually at puberty. This is the "vision quest" and it is a much anticipated event. The vision quest is no longer just for the Indian, as for a price a white participant can be lead through this truly grueling process.

The vision quest among the Miami Indians, as with most others, began with a fast of several days at puberty. This was for the distinct purpose of discovering their guardian spirit. Both boys and girl participated in this.

Fasting was just a part of it. There was a special place selected for the vision. It was always a lonely out of the way place where the seeker could be alone. In many tribes this was a pit in the ground away from the village and often on a hill so as to be nearer the Great Spirit.

A variation on the pit was given in *Kitchi-Gami,* where it is reported that, "The grandfather then took me by the hand and led me deep into the forest. Here he selected a lofty tree, a red pine, and prepared a bed for me in the branches on which I should lie down to fast. We cut down the bushes, and twined them through the pine branches. Then I plucked moss, with which I covered the trellis work, threw a mat my mother had made for the occasion over it, and myself on top of it. I was also permitted to fasten a few branches together over my head, as a sort of protection from wind and rain." It was imperative that the seeker does not break the fast. In the northeast it is so strictly adhered to that even swallowing a little rain water would ruin the quest.

The vision seeker was going to go through one of the most sacred of traditions. Through his quest he would, if successful, obtain a powerful medicine (or amulet) which would accompany him through all the trials of life.

Besides those preparations already mentioned, the seeker would sometimes take a sweat bath before hand for purification, as well as bathing in the smoke from pine kneedles. Depending on what tribe you belonged to you might then be painted with white clay, though this was not the rule. Usually after purification the seeker would go to his special spot naked save for moccasins and a breechclout so that he would be humbled before the Great Spirit.

The duration of the quest was anywhere from one to five days with four being the average. The visions were not always a success, but it was of great importance to not deceive others if you failed personally or the vision just did not come.

Again I turn to *Kitch-Gami* for an example. It is reported that, "I promised my grandfather that I would keep the fast, but unfortunately I did not keep my promise. For three days I bore the lying, and hunger, and thirst; but when I descended from the tree into the grass on the fourth day I saw refreshing leaves of a little herb growing near the tree. I could not resist it, but plucked the leaves and ate them. And when I had eaten them my craving grew so great that I walked about the forest, sought the edible sprigs, plants, mosses, and herbs I could find, and ate my fill."

This young boy slunk back to the grandfather, but was true enough of heart to admit his error. He was afraid of what reproach might await. But there was none, he was merely told that he would try again the next spring.

A great many people, skeptics who must find a rational explanation for everything, claim that the vision is manifested due to the hunger and state the seeker must be in after four and sometimes more days. But in point of fact this fasting process is part of the cleansing and is in fact not a great deal different from the Jewish/Christian custom of fasting for cleansing.

The lad that I spoke of from the work of *Kitchi-Gami* had indeed the next spring a very long quest, eight days! But the results finally came to him. His narrative is wonderful and says so much about the Indian spirituality and the vision quest itself.

The lad is simply called in the book, The Cloud. Here is the way The Cloud's vision occurred. He said that, "On the eighth night I heard a rustling and waving in the branches. It was like a heavy bear or elk breaking through the shrubs and forest. I was greatly afraid. But the man who approached me, whoever he may have been, read my thoughts and saw my fear at a distance; so he came towards me more and more gently, and rested, quite noiselessly, on the branches over my head. Then he began to speak to me and to ask me, 'Are you afraid my son?' 'No,' I replied, 'I know longer fear.' 'Why art thou here in this tree?' I replied, 'To fast to gain strength , and know my life."

The communication between The Cloud and the man was not in verbal utterings, but as though they looked into each others hearts and minds and knew the thoughts. The Cloud was instructed to follow the mysterious man.

The Cloud rose up from his bed with little effort, after eight nights and he followed. But I am sure he did not physically follow, rather in the spirit as this was his vision. His spirit floated towards the east. In fact, The Cloud said it felt as though they were floating on air, going higher, and higher into a lofty mountain ever eastward.

Cloud said, "When we reached the summit after a long time, I found a wigwam built there, into which we entered. At first I saw nothing but a large white stone that lay in the middle of the hut; but on looking around more sharply, I saw four men sitting around the stone. They invite me to take a seat on the white stone in the midst of them. But I hardly sat down and the stone began sinking into the earth. 'Stay!' one of the men said; 'wait a minute; we have forgotten the foundation.' Thus speaking he fetched a white tanned deer-skin, and covered the stone with it; when I sat down on it again, it was as firm as a tree, and I sat comfortably."

It is in such manner that the vision quest proceeds. The amazing thing to all who have studied this phenomenon is that it works. It should never be tried alone however as special instruction is required.

This chapter on dreams and visions can probably be best ended with a letter written in 1709 at Quebec by missionary Raudot. You must remember though that this will have a slant to his own way of thinking.

The letter begins, "The Indians are much given to dreams and are so well persuaded that it is their spirit who gives them to them, that they absolutely must carry them out. It is dreams which oblige them to undertake wars, to make great voyages, to abandon war parties which they have undertaken against their enemies and to return from them to their cabins. It is also these dreams that give them their spirit, or to use their term, their manito, which they imagine takes care of them in all the acts of their lives.

"The Indians whom time has made wise in spite of themselves and incapable of the same debauches that they formerly had, recount to their children of the ways they came into the world, of their country and their wars, and tell them a thousand stories filled with superstition. But as soon as there is one of them who has reached the age of ten or twelve years and who can use the bow and arrow, his father says to him that he is of an age to get a spirit and to choose a manito for himself, and he gives him at the same time the instructions necessary to succeed in this.

"For this purpose he has him "mattach" or paint his face black with crushed charcoal and requires him in this state to fast for several days, in order that, having the brain empty he can more easily dream during his sleep, which is the time that this god ought to disclose himself to him and strike his imagination with some extraordinary thing or some animal which holds the place of divinity for him. The father anxious to know the dream of this child, watches the time of his awakening in order that he speaks to no one before him and questions him privately on what happened in his imagination during the night; if nothing has appeared, he counsels him to continue his fast saying to him that on this occasion he must give marks of his firmness and his strength. Finally, his brain represents to him some object such as the sun, the thunder, or other extraordinary things of which he has often heard his father or elders speak.

"When this child dreams he runs to carry the news to his father, who strongly recommends to him not to divulge it and encourages him with many reasons to accept this dream and to honor this idea which he takes thenceforth from his childhood for his divinity, for his manito, for his protector, and continues during his life to worship it by sacrifices and by feasts which he gives in its honor."

Who dreams the dreams? They all do. The lowest person to the most noble chief to the prophets known as the Winkles, they all dream and they all have visions—and they are given powerful medicine from the manitous!

Chapter Nine: The Woodland Shaman Herbalist

In thinking about Indian religion and the shamanistic practices which are deeply rooted in the realm of spirits, we overlook an important and very practical function of the shaman. This is the shaman as a doctor of medicine, not the intangible (but often potent) spirit medicine. He was also a master of using that which grows around him to cure the ailings of the people charged to his care under com-mission of the Great Spirit.

Not far from the Late Woodland village site, Old Van Etten Creek which Kathy and I have been excavating, is a wonderful bog. This bog is really a shinning green gem for it is filled with the most useful of food and medicinal plants. It would be a veritable cornucopia to a shaman herbalist—and I suspect it was in the past.

Kathy, Mikie and I have named this pot shard bog, for it bears the evidence of its former human inhabitants. One day as I knelt beside the mirror like surface of the water, I stared past my reflection which seemed to merge with the sky above, and there were pieces of pottery laying in the water. Little bits of prehistory perhaps a millennium or more in age. From that point on this site became known as Pot Shard Bog.

It is at such places that we who are in tune with pulsations emanating from the past can be privy to what happened at a particular site. It is an unfortunate fact that modern archaeology has lost this unique ability. But allow me to paint a picture of what transpired by these pot shards over a thousand years ago, a story whispered in my ears by the winds, or perhaps the sacred breath of some long gone shaman.

Picture if you will, dawn breaking with fiery red brilliance over the pine forests of the northeast woodlands. The trees and the rising morning mists glowed with morning hues giving the entire setting around Pot Shard Bog a surrealistic countenance.

With cunning known to few he moved down from the village. His footsteps were soft and carefully chosen—not even the animals drinking from the bogs waters took notice of him.

The shadowed figure of the shaman herbalist knelt on the moist carpet of pine needles. A smile came to his lips as gently, almost erotically he touched the leaf of a small plant. The plant held no secrets from him. He plucked it and uttering a special thanks placed it in his medicine bag.

He knew the mysteries of the bog—he had studied them all his life. Because of his understanding of nature and herbs around him, he was able to provide his people with medicines that they required.

Plants rich in nutrients grow here, and he has taught the villagers about the food plants so they can receive the abundance which the Great Spirit has provided.

It is a sacred chain of events; knowledge divinely imparted to the shaman from the spirits, from the shaman to the people come medicine and food—thus health, and all this from the Great One Gitchi Manitou.

Before the slumber of the summer night passes by and the villagers awake, the shaman's search for medicinal roots and herbs is complete. Next to the bog he leaves an offering, a bit of tobacco and some broken shards of pottery—shards that seemed to transcend time to appear before me on that particular day.

At times the medicinal properties of plants come to the shaman in dreams. One such incident was reported in the book, *The Tree That Never Dies*, by Pamela J. Dobson. Ms. Dobson was interviewing an elderly Indian who told her, "My granddad, one time he was out hunting. He had sore eyes. He got so he couldn't see. Stayed in camp. Laid down. He said he went to sleep. He dreamed about a little flower, about three inches high, red flower on it, one flower is all there was on it. In his dream someone

came over and told him, 'Use that.' When he woke up he told his buddy what he dreamed. 'I wonder if you could find that out there?' 'I believe I could,' his friend replied. So his friend went out and got the flower. He put a little water in a pan and put the flower in the pan. I think it was the root of it. That's what he used in his eye to wash it. Couple of days he could see real good."

A chief root which was highly regarded by the shaman at the time of first contact with the Europeans was called Oscar. This was said to be a wonder cure for many things including wounds, ulcers and a wide variety of sores. Their were also many poisonous plants made use of and these seem to have been collectively refereed to as Ondachiera.

The shaman's medicine plants were, and are, very potent. It was reported by the Jesuits that a Frenchman had by accident eaten one of the poison roots, his situation was dire and he was taken to the shaman for healing.

The report states, "He became very ill at once and as pale as death, but he was cured by emetics which the shaman made him swallow. Again we had another apprehension, which afterward turned into a laughing matter. Some little Indians had some roots called Ooxrat, like a small turnip or chestnut, which they had just pulled up to take to their cabins. A young French boy, living with us, had asked for some and had eaten one or two. At first he found the taste rather agreeable, but shortly afterward he felt a great pain in his mouth, like a burning prickling flame, and a great quantity of secretion and phlegm continually dropped from his mouth so that he thought he was about to die. And in fact we did not know what to do about it."

The youngster was taken to the shaman who after having identified the plant consumed chuckled a little. This was a medicine that was used for good. These roots were used to purge phlegm and moisture in the head of old people and to clear the complexion! To avoid the burning sensation in the mouth they were cooked first.

There was a special and very potent concoction made by the shaman from the leaves of the common sumac and the root of an herb called Pallaganghy or Ocre. This compound was used to cure those who had been wounded in the chest, head or arm and who had lost much blood through the mouth. They are said to be cured in a short time.

The shaman used the very same cure for women who were troubled with having their monthly period. An early account states that, "They take an equal quantity of the sumac and the ocre, they crush the one and the other separately; after each is in powder they mix them together and put them in a small kettle on a few embers; they add to it two times as much of sumac berries and make the confined woman drink the warm water in which the whole is soaked until she is entirely cured. That is to say, the space of two or three days, each day replacing in the kettle a similar dose, and giving some of it to the patient to drink a little before she eats at noon at four o'clock and in the evening before retiring, the blood comes after the second or third taking, sometimes coagulated and as big as the fist, sometimes putrid, and other times drop by drop."

The shaman used this same cure for those suffering from dropsy, but they would not eat any of the medicine rather they would just drink the water it had been soaking in.

Again this cure was used for mouth injuries. They were cured by the medicine being held on the gums. The bark from the root of the cherry tree was also chewed and held on the affected gums to cure disorders.

The shaman would use the above concoction minus the sumac berries in order to cure venereal disease.

It seems that no job was to big for the shaman, of course this depended on the amount of his training. No matter how magnificent he or she performed the early whites were ready to leap upon him coals of fire for his "wicked ways."

Again I would like to quote an early source as to the power of these men of the Great Spirit. The document says, "When one is wounded by a gun shot, or arrow, or fall, or when one has been crushed under a tree, they use a root that they call by the generic word Ouissoucatcki, that is to say, with several feet; they crush this root and put four pinches of it with a quill in a little warm water that they make the patient swallow, who is marvelously strengthened by this medicine. If he is in a delirium he returns to good sense, and the blood that he vomits begins to stop; when he has breathed a little they give him some of that which we have shown to stop the blood entirely and for the perfect cure."

The shaman would use the root of the akiskiouraoui as a remedy for being bitten by a poisonous snake. He also knows that the root of the wild chervil is excellent for the eyes. The root is steeped and then the water is dropped into the eye.

An early missionary compiled a list of common cures used by the shaman's of the northeastern woodland. Some of these cures include green earth or clay used for blood issuing from the abdomen. Four pills of this were taken in the morning and four in the evening.

The shaman boiled the root of the basswood for burns. The bark or leaves of the white oak were boiled for wounds. The bark of young pine trees was boiled for burns and wounds. The root of onis was boiled for all sorts of wounds.

To draw a connection between Pot Shard Bog and all of this, roots and herbs were found by me to be growing at the bog. It is my contention that they were also growing there in prehistory, and my gut feeling that they were certainly used by shaman's of those long ago days. Also it comes to mind that perhaps the reason so many whites have put the cures of the shaman's down as bunk is because they don't realize that it is often sacred music and chants which releases the power of these medicines.

The list, however, continues. The shaman used the root of the leather wood boiled for all sorts of wounds. It was also seen by early whites that it had properties which cured some forms of cancer! So intrigued were the French by this wood that they transported specimens back to their homeland for study. Though it is uncertain the leather wood spoken of is believed to be Dirca palustris.

Sarsaparilla root was applied for sores and cuts. The root and bark of the elder was used for a person failing in his limbs. This was boiled and a little was put into soup.

Let's just quickly run down the list of cures the shamans used;

Ginger—crushed into a powder for putting a stop to the pains of child birth.

Plant of a Thousand Leaves—Used for all manner of cuts.

Pine Branches—boiled and used for venereal disease.

Litre Leaf—Boiled and used for eye soreness.

Crushed Clam Shells—Blown into the eyes to remove films.

The White Creeper—For venereal disease.

Sumac—For looseness of bowels.

Bean Trefoil—For looseness of the bowls or a bloody issue. This was boiled and drank, and nothing else could be drank

Ash Bark—was chewed and then applied to sprains.

Bear Spleen—This was used to cure a toothache, though I doubt the pain was any worse than the cure.

But these, as well as others, are wonderful cures which were relayed through special people. People who knew their destiny from the time of their youth at their vision quest. As I stated, though, the cures were often made out as fake by the early Jesuits. The average European mind, in case you have not noticed, does not see the world as the Indian mind. Everything has a spirit in their sight, and you must know the manitou of a plant in order to unleash its power.

Because of this offerings were often left at the time plants were being collected. The shaman was so careful not to offend or disrupt the nature of things, that even in hunting a very rare herb he would pass up three or four plants only to pick the fifth. This made certain that there would indeed be future generations of this herb.

Let it not be thought that the cure to be effected was a simple matter or mixing herbs and music with sacred chantings. It was not! Allouez wrote a description of various cures performed by the shaman that no doctor of our day would ever try—because it is self sacrificing. The following quotation is from the *Jesuit Relations of 1675*. Allouez wrote:

"There exists in this country a species of idolatry; for, besides the head of the wild ox, with its horns, which they keep in their cabins to invoke, they possess bearskins, stripped from the head and not cut open in the middle. They leave on them the head, the eyes, and the snout, which they usually paint green. The head is raised on a pole in the mid-

dle of their cabin, the remainder of the skin hanging along the pole to the ground. They invoke it in their sicknesses, wars, and other necessities."

In this next passage remember that this is an early Jesuit writing and his views are thus slanted by his own beliefs, but the entire text to follow is important to understand the depth the shaman would go to in order to help those in his charge.

Deliette wrote, "Most often they don't cure the sick, although assuredly they have admirable drugs. It is only mere chance when they succeed. In the healing of wounds some of them are very skillful. I have seen them cure some surprising ones and in very short time. The sucking process, which they all practice, has no doubt a large share in this success. However full of puss a wound may be, they clean it out entirely without inflicting much pain. They take the precaution of putting a little powder in their mouths; but when they have drawn off the worst of it they no longer do so, but continue to suck at the wound until it appears ruddy, after which they chew up some medicine which they spit upon the wound merely wrapping up the whole day, while leaving the wound to suppurate. At night they wrap it also."

This chapter is about the shaman as an herbalist, however, I would be remiss if I did not share with you the following which continues Deliette's narrative, "When a man has been wounded by a gunshot or by an arrow through the body, at the bottom of the neck or opposite a rib, they open his side, after taking care to raise the skin a little so that on being lowered again the opening will be between two ribs. They pour into him a quantity of warm water, in which they have diluted some of their drugs, after which they have the patient make motions and inhale , and sometimes they even take hold of him by the arms and legs, pushing him to and fro between them, and then making him eject all this water through his wound, expelling along with it fragments of clotted blood, which otherwise, doubtless would suffocate him. Then they sprinkle him with some of their powdered herbs, which they put into their mouths, as I have said already, and they never close up the wound by day. I have seen two men who were healed this way."

The shaman was, as we have seen, a spiritualist, an herbalist, and from the above a physical therapist. To deviate on a familiar old phrase, he had to wear a headdress of many different feathers. There are those who considered his powers evil and discounted the contact period shaman as "witches."

The description in its true seance of the word is inaccurate. Yes they had powers which came from many different sources, but what convinced early missionaries that they were evil is that sometimes the shaman's powers were used to revenge wrongs done to his people. But this was a natural protective instinct.

Charievoix had the following to say about the Illinois shaman, "Among the Illinois and almost all the other nations, they make small figures to represent those whose days they have a mind to shorten, and which they stab to the heart. At other times they take a stone, and by means of certain invocations, they pretend to form such another in the heart of their enemy."

When Kathy and I began excavations at Old Van Etten Creek years ago I had an inborn respect for the culture that dwelt there, and for the remnant of that culture—but really other than what the artifacts told us, we knew little about these people. As I walk through this site now, I look at the village floor with a new respect for I can begin more to imagine what these people were like as I piece together bits of evidence about their shamanistic religion and their healing arts and talents.'

Chapter Ten: Mummies and Shamans of the Frozen North

The central focus of this book has been on the Indians of the eastern woodlands and the plains. Now I would like to drastically change direction and take you on a mysterious journey to the Aleutian Islands. This area is of particular interest because of the unique religious and shamanistic practices.

If the religious system of the woodlands and plains are a positive, and I have tried to portray them as such, then those of the Aleutian Islands and the Eskimo Indians in general is a sort of negative. You see their belief system is every bit as spirit oriented as other Indian cultures, but the driving force to them is fear. Of course, this is not difficult to understand when you consider how this culture evolved. It grew out of the harsh, unrelenting starkness of the environment, and it is definitely worth taking a close look at.

The shaman in the frozen northern tribes is called the "angutkoks." He is every bit as powerful as in other Indian cultures. He had the familiar powers to heal, commune with the spirits, see into the future and so on.

Harold McCraken wrote a wonderful, though now obscure book in the 1930's, detailing his expedition to the Aleutian Islands in search of legendary frozen mummies. He encountered the angutkoks first hand.

McCracken told that, at that time, very few whites had even spent an entire winter on the Diomede Islands. A friend of his was married to an Eskimo, and had been for over a year. Displaying how secretive these people are concerning their religion, despite the man's fairly long standing in the community, he was still considered an outsider when it came to the practices of the shaman.

McCracken said of the man, "At attempting to crash the gate at one of their parties when a medi-

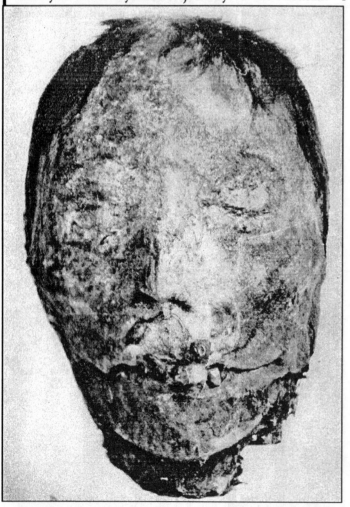

Headshot of Arctic mummy found by McCracken expedition.

cine man or angutkok was displaying his clandestine art, they seriously threatened his life when he attempted to remain after being told to get out of the place."

The shaman as McCracken found him in the 1920's was the greatest source of power in a given community, surpassing even the chieftain. They all feel humble before the shaman for the unbridled control he held over the spirit world. This seems a direct contrast to other Indian cultures where the shaman was pretty much controlled by the spirits around him—he was more or less an oracle of the spirits.

In his book, *God's Frozen Children,* Harold McCraken stated that the natives put in the shaman, complete faith over sickness and health, good and bad luck, the complex operations of nature, life and death, things both tangible and intangible—all these are subject to his mere whim and command.

A peculiar aspect of the arctic shaman's existence is the "life change." I have not run across this in other Indian culture or traditions. In the old days this was accomplished by stabbing a knife into his own heart, in the new ways a rifle bullet is shot through his heart. Of course death is imminent and it was reported that as the shaman fell to the ground that blood would pour fourth from the wound and from the mouth.

In a short space of time, usually within a half hour the lifeless body begins to regain consciousness. There are convulsions and "walrus like" grunts as the body begins to breath. At this point it is believed that a new spirit has taken up residence in the shaman's body.

Excavations at the tomb site.

According to the historic record, it is believed that the shaman can do this as often as he wishes, and in fact it is no more an ordeal to him than changing his clothes.

Mr. McCraken also explained that not only is the shaman impervious to the knife blade, but also to forms of death. For example they could survive execution by hanging, experiencing only a ten or twenty minuet "vacation" to the land of spirits before resuscitating.

The shaman of the frozen lands could also grant life over death to any person he wanted to. A particularly strong example follows: "If a native has a very violent pain in his abdomen he can go to the angutkok for treatment. To cure the ailment he is said to cut the patient's body wide open, remove the affected organs much as one might take apart a mechanical contrivance, clean them thoroughly, then replace them and send the patient away completely relieved of pain."

The shaman is, of course, just as capable of inflicting illness as curing it. The shaman of the Diomede Islands used an amulet shaped like a small spindle of ivory. It was highly polished, but was not carved. Casting a spell with this little device was quite simple, if you had the spirit power. An incantation was muttered over it, then it was thrown out into the winter night and its spell was thus cast.

Not unlike the medicine bundle of the plains and northeast woodland, a necessary part of the shaman's work was a medicine kit. The kit typically contained an elliptical shaped box, about fifteen inches long and made from driftwood. Wood other than driftwood was a rare and precious commodity. The box was likely to contain the mummified remains of several sea birds which were encased in walrus intestine and decorated with fur. Also included were the mummified heads of birds and fur cut into various shapes. Small items of carved ivory were common as well a polar bears teeth. The kit was said to be able to cure most anything.

To understand the unwavering faith that was put in these shamans, one must understand the hostile climate these natives lived in. McCracken after his expedition to the Diomede Islands wrote an unparalleled description which will help you to comprehend.

He wrote, "Throughout most of the summer

the section is shrouded in heavy murky fogs almost as dense as smoke, or torn by terrific gales that lash the sea into murderous havoc. Throughout the winter the great fields of floating ice that cover the center of the Arctic top of the earth, jam through the narrow gateway between the two continents like a vast heard of stampeding prehistoric mammoths, all struggling to surge through a narrow rocky canyon at the same time. The power of the universe is behind the ice. Great bergs are literally ground to snow. The ridge and the moraines creep and twist like a serpentine thing alive, and moan and groan like a creature in the throes of death. The power of it appears to be irresistible. Yet the two little Diomede Islands for many centuries have proudly raised their barren rocky heads in the very center of it, where it's power is the greatest, boldly to defy it."

The death customs of these Native Americans reflect the climate in which they live. When a villager died he was carried out of the village naked, and laid on the rocks behind the village where he was torn to pieces and devoured by the village dogs. Naturally then, more emphasis was placed on the spiritual being than the physical. This of course is true, but the spirits of the dead, even though of one loved during life are thought to be malicious trouble makers and are held with the greatest of fear!

There is a land of the spirits, or souls, but little is on record about that place. It seems not to be the tranquil place adhered to by other tribes, nor does the spirit necessarily go there.

One Eskimo told explorer/ethnologist Edward Weyer, "We believe that men live on after death here on earth, for we often see the dead in our dream fully alive." Here again we find great faith placed in the dream world. Wyler suggests that this is due to the fact that sleep to the native closely resembles death.

For now let's return to the shaman. It is a common belief among the tribes of Eskimos that when a soul is sick, or lost, a person can obtain a new one. The shaman can secure this from an animal, or even a child! It is also believed that fragments of the soul from time to time go astray and these can be collected by the shaman and reused.

When a child was sick it was not, in times past, an uncommon practice for the soul to be removed and placed in some sort of an amulet for safe keep-

ing. To further protect this soul the shaman may put the amulet in his medicine bag.

Among the Iglulik's there was believed an extra measure of protection for the soul if at birth it is taken from the child by the shaman and placed under the mothers lamp and left there as long as the child lives.

I don't think that any other group of people so blatantly profess the authority over the other world so as to resurrect the dead. There is unconditional faith in the shaman to preform this task with relative ease.

Weyer told of a strange case, "This is the tale of Akarak, a Kilusiktok Eskimo. A spirit or the malignant shade of a dead man struck him on the nape of the neck while he was hunting south of Bathurst Inlet. He fell dead into the swamp and his face was buried in the water. There at sunset his son found him; his face was blue, his hands were frozen stiff and his body was cold and dead. The son caught hold of his ring finger with one hand and extended the arm, then laid his other hand on Akarak's shoulder. Forthwith the latter's soul returned to his body and he was restored to life again. As soon as they arrived in camp the shamans invoked their magic powers and restored the hunter to health. Akarak had been a fairly powerful shaman before his adventure and his prestige was greatly augmented after this incident."

Another account worth looking at was told to Vilhjalmur Stefansson. He was told by a native, "We ourselves can raise people from the dead. You know some years before you first came to the Mackenzie district, Taiakpanna died. He died in the morning,

Two face masks from the tomb.

and Alualnk, the great shaman, arrived in the afternoon. The body of Taiakpanna was still laying there in the house; Alualuk immediately summoned his familiar spirits, performed the appropriate ceremonies, and woke Taiakpanna from the dead, and, as you know, he is still living."

Paradise, as I already stated, is not a place commonly believed in by the Eskimo. Their vision of life after death is rather somber, and although the spirit is believed to live on earth, there is also a special place for the spirit to go—though it is not (!) considered a "paradise."

Death opens the gate to a vague, gloomy place where no joy and gladness is known. Dreadful thoughts of death preoccupied their minds always, which in itself seems a little odd for a culture that attests to so many resurrections.

In his book, *The Eskimo,* Edmund Weyer explained, "The Eskimos of the Bearing Strait believe that the shades of shamans and of such as die by accident, violence, or starvation, go to a land of plenty in the sky, where there is light, food, and water in abundance; while the shades of people who die from normal causes go to the underground land of the dead, where they depend entirely upon the offerings of food, water, and clothing made to them by the relatives. Even in the land of plenty, shades can be made happier by being remembered with presents."

If you recall, in the northeast woodlands the soul of the departed is said to linger around the grave for four days. In most Eskimo cultures the

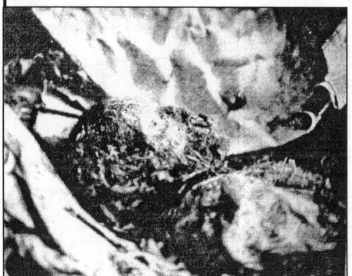

Head & shoulders of the mummy.

soul lingers around the house for five days—but here there is once more a vast difference in beliefs between areas. Rather than then going to the land of the souls (such as it is with this culture), the soul stands by its grave until it is called upon to enter into a newborn child. Thus we see a form of belief in reincarnation. The soul then remains with the child until death. This is not a pure form of reincarnation however as this soul acts as a guardian, not unlike a guardian spirit.

Such aversion to death and to the dead was not always the case among those dwelling Aleutian Islands. If you recall, I said that Harold McCracken's expedition was to find mummies in the area of the Aleutians. In fact he discovered a burial culture that was comparable in complexity to any of those found in the woodlands, plains, or mounds of the southeastern United States.

McCracken and his entourage landed on a small, remote island after examined many such islands. Their hopes were drawing slim of ever finding the objects of their search. However, many artifacts of ancient vintage were seen to be falling out of the banks on this particular atoll, so they began doing excavations.

A member of the party named Bird after a while gave a loud report, "I have found a cabin!"

I quote from McCracken's account, "Gathering up my handful of finds and dragging my shovel, I went over to where he knelt pawing the earth out from under the overhanging sod. He was grinning broadly, though a bit uncertainly, as I came up.

"I sat down beside him and peered into the hole which he had dug. My heart gave a sudden jump and I could plainly see a row of age rotted logs; and the manner in which they were closely fitted together assured me immediately that they had been carefully placed there by human hands—apparently a long time ago. We started digging the earth away."

What Bird had busted his way into was an ancient tomb which was about to reveal much about the customs of the ancestors of those currently inhabiting the harsh islands.

What was uncovered was a structure that was quite well built, and was about nine feet wide. Understand that this had to be an important person buried here to have a tomb constructed of wood, a very rare commodity in this area except for drift wood!

When the company removed the top layer of logs, they found beneath that a layer of rotting grass mats. Many grave goods were found which would accompany the deceased into the next world, which by the looks of things was far more promising than most Eskimos assumed it would be.

Oil lamps were found as well as much woven grass matting and many seal skins. There were also bidarka paddles, a repair kit assumed to have been placed their for the spirit boat which would carry the deceased to the next world.

Again I will return to McCracken's own words to describe the actual sarcophagus, "There was an unspoken sense of reverence for the mighty Aleut chieftain or hunter for whom it was now apparent this primitively elegant structure had been built.

"The box like structure was divided into two equal compartments. One compartment, it appeared, contained a single wrapped body. The other contained several bodies, less meticulously wrapped and much crowded together."

Placed over the chieftain was a large bundle of heavy harpoon shafts, and each is said to have been tipped with bone harpoons. There was also present a wooden shield.

There was a container for each body that was made of tanned and decorated pup-seal skins which were attached to wooden hoops by thongs. These containers laid on a lining of sea-otter skin of which the entire tomb had been lined! Other spaces were filled with clothing and various personal belongings. Next to the chief laid a wooden hat of a type used for festive occasions. Close to him were personal items which included a parka made of sea otter and trimmed with bird skins. There was a small carving that looked to have been made of pure marble. This little carving was identified as a plug worn through a hole in the lower lip. There was also a shallow wooden bowl at the body's feet, flint tools, rolls of fine woven grass fabric and various sundry odds and ends.

McCracken then stated, "We loosened the sinew ropes which bound the container of the chieftain and carefully laid back the outer fabric and skin coverings, and unwound the finer shroud of grass fabrics and gut. Suddenly the first conclusive evi-dence of our triumph sprang into view—a dry, brown, wrinkled hand. Almost breathlessly I touched it. It was as hard as dry leather—the hand of a stone age human mummy of the Arctic!"

The chief was of small stature, and like so many ancient Indians practiced, he had been placed in a fetal position. The chief was clad in a magnificent parka of sea otter which was trimmed much like the one already described. One oddity noted is that the finger nails had been pulled out. This was a practice common in Egyptian mummification. Besides that portions of the anatomy had been removed and filled with grass so that he would retain a certain fullness that he had in mortal life. The eye balls had been removed and the sockets filled with brown clay.

McCracken noted that he had been laid flat on a second wooden shield in the manner of the Vikings. So found here were elements of two other ancient cultures who could have possibly influenced these ancient Native Americans.

It is assumed that those buried with the chieftain were his servants in life. They were to accompany him to the next world and aid him there much as Ushatis accompanied the noted Egyptian mummies. Oddly enough one of these grave escorts was wearing beads later identified as Korean amber! McCracken felt that these crudely drilled and strung beads proved a contact between the aboriginal Americans and Asia.

One can not deny that this was a unique and highly significant find which has revealed much about the spiritual beliefs of the ancient forefathers

Lifting the mummy from the tomb.

of the Eskimo.

But there is more to be said about the Eskimo and their feelings on the dead and spirits. I am afraid I drifted away from that for a moment.

One last quote from this particular area which again shows a certain peculiarity of customs. Weyer in his book, "The Eskimo" (1932) stated that, "According to Eskimo belief, one cause of sickness is possession by an evil spirit. If efforts fail to placate the evil spirit or to exorcise it from the body, the patient grows weaker and approaches death. It is then obvious that the cause of the disease is more powerful than human expedients, and that the malicious spirit is a dangerous force not to be thwarted."

It is considered a great risk to even come in contact with a person who is dead or dying for fear of being contaminated by the evil. Some went to the extent of preparing the body for the grave before death occurred do they could avoid touching it later. Some even carried the person who was near death to an abandoned hut and left the person there to die of neglect.

To prevent the corpse from moving after death and also to restrict the spirit, the body was tightly bound.

The Eskimo culture seems an exercise in futility except for their noble descent as indicated by the mummified remains which McCracken found, and their extremely powerful shamans. Shamans of all the Indian cultures have great powers imparted on them by the world of the spirits yet none seem so powerful as these shamans of North America's frozen regions.

Face masks play an important part in the shamanistic practices of the Eskimo. In fact, the art of carving masks probably became more advanced among the Eskimo than other tribes. This was due to the simple fact that after each ceremony the masks were destroyed and new ones had to be created for each ceremony. They got a lot of practice.

Weyer reported, "They are utilized in two ways: in actual ceremonies and as funeral properties. Their utilization in ceremonies is the more important purpose, both among the Eskimo and their Indian neighbors.

Petitot mentions the use of masks by the Tinneh Indians in games and at the interment of the dead. In the Aleutian Islands and thence eastward masks have figured prominently in ceremonial observances, and have sometimes been employed for funeral purposes. The characteristic Aleut mask has a crosspiece on the inside that is clenched between the teeth."

Like their Indian brothers, the Eskimo believes that everything has a spirit. The shamans give visualization to these elusive forms through the masks they can create.

The myths of the Eskimo people seem as allegorical as those of the main stream Indian. Take for example their legend as to the creation of the sun and the moon. It is believed that these heavenly orbs were at one time brother and sister. The boy chased the girl and both of them were swept off into the sky, where the boy became the moon and his sister the sun.

Weyer reported that thunder was believed to originate by spirits rubbing together hides. Rain has a very fanciful origin too, Weyer said that, "Rain is occasioned by a lake in heaven overflowing; and snow is the blood of the dead, or chips of the narwhal tusk carved by the moon. The natives of Selawik account for snowfall in a different way; the sky is a land like the earth but hanging upside down, with the grass growing downward; and when the wind blows the grass is stirred and the snow is sifted to the earth. Furthermore, there are a myriad of lakes in the sky and at night these shine and appear as stars. In northwest Alaska and Coronation Gulf shooting stars are thought to be star dung!"

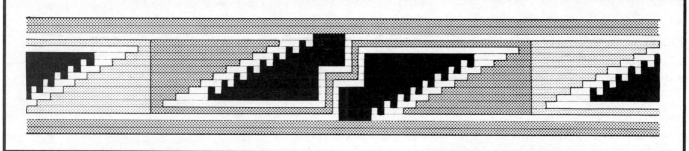

Chapter Eleven: Great Myths of the Great Northeast

The spiritual mythology of the American Indian is among the most colorful to be found anywhere in the world. In it are clues to the secret inner workings of their shamanism and ritual beliefs. An Ottawas legend, for example, titled, "The Worship of the Sun," incorporates many areas of belief. It encompasses the vision quest, celestial spirit dweller, intervention of the spirits in the lives of mortals, shamanism, and for appeasing the spirits—ritualistic sacrifice.

"The Worship of the Sun," is vibrant and alive with tradition which is preserved in an allegorical style. This particular legend was recorded by Henry R. Schoolcraft in his 1851, "The American Indian." As it is here presented, see how many of the elements I named that you can pick out.

"A long time ago there lived an aged Odjibwa and his wife, on the shore of Lake Huron. They had only a son, a very beautiful boy, whose name was O-na-wut-a-qut-o, or he that catches the clouds. The family were of the totem of the beaver. The parents were very proud of him, and thought to make him a celebrated man, but when he reached the proper age, he would not submit to the We-koon-dewin, or

fast. When this time arrived, they gave him charcoal instead of his breakfast, but he would not blacken his face. If they denied him food he would look for birds eggs, along the shore, or pick up the heads of fish that had been cast away, and boil them. One day, they took away violently the food he had thus prepared, and cast him some coals in place of it. This act brought him to a decision. He took the coals and blackened his face and went out of the lodge. He did not return, but slept without; and during the night he had a dream. He dreamed that he saw a very beautiful female come down from the clouds and stand by his side. '0-na-wut-a-qut-o,' she said, 'I am come for you—step in my tracks.' The young man did so, and presently felt himself ascending above the tops of the trees—he mounted up, step by step, into the air, and through the clouds. His guide, at length, passed through an orifice, and he, following her, found himself standing on a beautiful plain.

"A path led to a splendid lodge. He followed her into it. It was large, and divided into two parts. On one end he saw bows and arrows, clubs and spears, and various warlike implements tipped with silver. On the other end were things belonging specifically to females. This was the home of his fair guide, and he saw that she had, on the frame, a broad rich belt, of many colors, which she was weaving. She said to him, 'My brother is coming and I must hide you.' Presently the brother came in, very richly dressed, and shining as if he had points of silver all over him. He took down from the wall a splendid pipe, together with his sack of a-pa-ko-ze-gun, or smoking mixture. When he had finished regaling himself in this way, and laid his pipe aside, he said to his sister; 'Nemissa,' (which is my elder sister) 'when will you quit these practices? Do you forget that the Greatest of the Spirits has commanded that you should not take away the children from below? Perhaps you suppose that you have concealed 0-na-wut-a-qut-o, but do I not know of his coming? If you would not offend me, send him back immediately.' But this address did not alter her purpose. She would not send him back. Finding that she was purposed in her mind, he then spoke to the young lad, and called him from his hiding place. 'Come out of your concealment, and walk about and amuse yourself. You will grow hungary if you

remain there.' He then presented him with bow and arrows, and a pipe of red stone, richly ornamented. This was taken as the word of consent to his marriage; so the two were considered husband and wife from that time.

"0-na-wut-a-qut-o found everything exceedingly fair and beautiful around him, but he found no inhabitants except her brother. There were flowers on the plains. There were bright and sparkling streams. There were green valleys and pleasant trees. There were gay birds and beautiful animals, but they were not such as he had been accustomed to see. There was also day and night as on the earth; but he observed the brother regularly left the lodge, and remained absent all day long; and every evening the sister departed, though it was commonly but for part of the night.

"His curiosity was aroused to solve this mystery. He obtained the brother's consent to accompany him on one of his daily journeys. They traveled over a smooth plain without boundaries, until 0-nawut-a-qut-o felt the gnawings of appetite, and asked his companion if there was no game. 'Patience! my brother. We shall soon reach the spot where I eat my dinner, and you will then see how I am provided. After walking on a long time they came to a place which was spread over with fine mats, where they sat down to refresh themselves. There was, at this place, a hole in the sky; and 0-na-wut-a-qut-o looked down at the bidding of his companion upon the earth. He saw below the great lakes, and the villages of the Indians. In one place, he saw a war party stealing on the camp of their enemies. In another, he saw feasting and dancing. On a green plain young men were playing at ball. Along a stream, women were employed in gathering the apuk-wa for mats.

"'Do you see,' said the brother, 'that group of children playing beside a lodge. Observe that beautiful and active boy, he said, at the same time darting something at him from his hand. The child immediately fell, and was carried into the lodge.

"They looked again and saw the people gathering about the lodge. They heard the she-she-gwan of the meeta, and the song he sung, asking that the child's life might be spared. To this request, the companion of 0-na-wut-a-qut-o made answer— 'send me up the sacrifice of a white dog.' Immediately a feast was ordered by the parents of the child, the white dog was killed, his carcass was roasted, and all the wise men and medicine men of the village assembled to witness the ceremony. "There are many below,' continued the voice of the brother, 'whom you call great in medical skills, but it is because their ears are open, and they listen to my voice, that they are able to succeed. When I have struck one with sickness, they direct the people to look to me; and when they send me the offering I ask, I remove my hand from off them, and they are well.' After he had said this, they saw the sacrifice parceled out in dishes, for those who were at the feast. The master of the feast then said, 'we send this to the Great Manitou,' and immediately the roasted animal came up. Thus their dinner was supplied, and after they had eaten, they returned to the lodge by another way.

"After this manner they lived for some time; but the place became wearisome at last. 0-no-wut-a-qut-o thought of his friends, and wished to go back to them. He had not forgotten his native village and his father's lodge; and he asked leave of his wife, to return. At length she consented. 'Since you are better pleased with the cares and ills, and the poverty of the world, than with the peaceful delights of the sky, and its boundless prairies, go! I give you permission, and since I have brought you hither, I will conduct you back; but remember, you are still my husband, I hold a chain in my hand by which I can draw you back whenever I will. My power over you is not in any manner diminished. Beware, therefore, how you venture to take a wife among the people below. Should you ever do so, it is then that you should feel the force of my displeasure.'

As she said this, her eyes sparkled—she raised herself slightly on her toes, and stretched herself up, with a majestic air; and at that moment, 0-no-wut-a-qut-o awoke from his dream. He found himself on the ground near his father's lodge, at the very spot he had laid himself down to fast. Instead of the bright beings of a higher world, he found himself surrounded by parents and relatives. His mother told him he had been absent a year. The change was so great that he remained for some time moody and abstracted, but by degrees, he recovered his spirits. He began to doubt the reality of all he had heard and seen above. At last he forgot the admonitions of

his spouse, and married a beautiful young woman of his own tribe. But within four days she was a corpse. He repeated the offense by a second marriage. Soon afterward he went out of the lodge, one night, but never returned. It was believed that his wife had recalled him to the region of the clouds, where the tradition asserts, he still dwells, and walks on the daily rounds which he once witnessed."

This story brings a great deal of understanding of the Indians view of the spiritual word and its influence on man. In a previous chapter I told you about a "Path of Souls" to the west which leads to Paradise. The place where 0-no-wut-a-qut-o was transported to during his year long vision quest appears to be a paradisiacal state, but not the same one.

Entry to this realm or dimension was gained through some sort of "orifice". This in turn reminds me of the great hexagon mound group of Newark, Ohio. Discussed earlier, this is an earthwork which shows the path of life from the womb through the afterlife.

Many cultures, including the Jews in the Old Testament of the Holy Bible, taught that intermarriage with spirit beings did in fact take place. This story graphically illustrates that the concept of human/spirit bonding was a part of American Indian religious beliefs.

The brother in this story was a Great Manitou and his countenance was quite brilliant. I am reminded of the little spirit helpers which blazed with fiery brilliance in the chapter on the Shaking Tents. This manitou was dressed in the finest and sparkled with points of light all over him. His over all look sounds quite extraterrestrial.

Most interesting to me is the manner in which the Great Manitou held the fate of the mortals in his hands. It is easy to understand through this why animal sacrifice was indeed, and still is in fact, practiced among the Indians. It was to care for the needs of the spirits dwelling above, and all around them.

There are many Indian traditions about the celestial or sky beings. The Indians of the northeast woodlands had a story often told around their campfires which is called, "The Lone Lightning." Here again an earth dweller is lead up to the abode of the sacred sky people, the manitous.

The story begins, "A little orphan boy who had

no one to care for him, was once living with his uncle, who treated him very badly, making him do hard things, and giving him very little to eat, so that the boy pined away, he never grew much, and became, through hard usage, very thin and light. At last the uncle felt ashamed of this treatment, and determined to make amends for it, by fattening him up, but his real object was to kill him by over feeding. He told his wife to give the boy plenty of bear's meat, and to let him have the fat, which is thought to be the best part. They were both very assiduous in cramming him, and one day came near choking him to death by forcing the fat down his throat. The boy escaped and fled from the lodge. He knew not where to go, but wandered about. When night came on, he was afraid the wild beasts would eat him, so he climbed up into the forks of a high pine tree, and there he fell asleep in the branches, and had an aupoway, or ominous dream.

"A person appeared to him from the upper sky, and said, 'My poor little lad, I pity you, and the bad usage you have received from your uncle has led me to visit you: follow me, step in my tracks.' Immediately his sleep left him, and he rose up and followed his guide, mounting up higher and higher into the air, until he reached the upper sky. Here twelve arrows were put into his hands, and he was told that there were a great many manitous in the northern sky, against whom he must go to war, and try to waylay and shoot them. Accordingly, he went to that part of the sky, and, at long intervals, shot arrow after arrow, until he had expended eleven in a vain attempt to kill the manitous. At the flight of each arrow there was a long and solitary streak of lightening in the sky—then all was clear again, and not a cloud or spot could be seen. The twelfth arrow he held a long time in his hands, and looked around keenly on every side to spy the manitous he was after. But these manitous were very cunning, they could change their form in a moment. All they feared was the boy's arrows, for these were magic arrows, which had been given to him by a good spirit, and had power to kill them, if correctly aimed. At length, the boy drew up his last arrow, settled in his aim, and let fly, as he thought, into the very heart of the chief of the manitous; but before the arrow reached him, he changed himself into a rock. Into this rock the arrow sank deep and stuck fast.

" 'Now your gifts are all expended,' cried the enraged manitou, 'and I will make an example of your audacity and pride of heart, for lifting your bow against me.' And so saying he transformed the boy into Nazhik-a-wa-wa-sun, or Lone Lightning, which may be observed in the northern sky to this day."

There is a tradition in the northeast woodland, which is as far as I can determine, rather unique to this culture. That tradition is the duality of the soul. The Eskimo taught that the soul could be fragmentary, but this is a little different. There was a certain shaman among the Algonquins who lived during the early 1800's. While explaining burial customs to the curious he explained this duality of the soul.

This shaman explained that coverings were (and still are) built over graves to shed rain. These, in former times, were constructed of cedar bark. The structure is roof shaped and looks very much like a small house. At the head end an opening is cut, this was for the soul to come and go at will.

The interviewer inquired as to why if the soul left the body at death and went to Paradise, then why would it also be present at the grave.

The old shaman explained, "There are two souls. You know that in dreams we pass over countries, and see hills and lakes and mountains, and many scenes which pass before our eyes and affect us. Yet at the same time our bodies do not stir, and there is a soul left with the body, else it would be dead. So you perceive, it must be another soul that accompanies us."

Of all the traditions of the northeast woodland culture, my personal favorite is that of, "The Magician of Lake Huron." Here again we find many spiritual concepts present. Most interesting is this great shaman's, named Masswaweinni, prowess in dealing with the spirits around him. This story also contains the tradition of how corn was brought to the people. Corn was an all important crop as the Indian learned agriculture, and indeed this food staple was worshiped by many as a sort of manna from heaven.

According to the story, "At the time that the Ottowas inhabited the Manitoline Islands, in Lake Huron, there was a famous magician or shaman living amongst them whose name was Masswaweinini, or the Living Statue. It happened, by the fortune of war, that the Ottowa tribe were driven off that chain of islands by the Iroquois, and obliged to flee away to the country laying between Lake Superior and the Upper Mississippi, to the banks of a lake called, Lake of the Cut-ears. But the shaman Masswaweinini remained behind on the wide stretching and picturesque Manatoulines, a group of islands which had been deemed from the earliest times, a favorite residence of the manitous. His object was to act as a sentinel to his country men, and keep a close watch on their enemies, the Iroquois, that he might give timely information of their movements. He had with him two boys; with their aid he paddled stealthily around the shores, kept himself secreted in nooks and bays, and hauled up his canoe every night, into the thick woods, and carefully obliterated his tracks upon the sand.

"One day he rose very early, and started on a hunting excursion, leaving the boys asleep, and limiting himself to the thick woods, lest he should be discovered. At length he unexpectedly came to the borders of an extensive open plain. After gazing around him, and seeing no one, he directed his steps across it, intending to strike the opposite side of it; while travelling, he discovered a man of small stature, who appeared suddenly on the plain before him, and advanced to meet him. He wore a red feather on his head, and coming up with a familiar air, accosted Masswaweinini by name, and said gaily, 'Where are you going?' He then took out his smoking apparatus, and invited him to smoke. 'Pray,' he said, while thus engaged, 'wherein does your strength lie?' 'My strength,' answered Masswaweinini, 'is similar to the human race, and common to the strength given to them, and no stronger.' 'We must wrestle,' said the man of the red feather. 'If you should make me fall, you will say to me, I have thrown you, Wa-ge-me-na.'

"As soon as they had finished smoking and put up their pipe, the wrestling began. For a long time the strife was doubtful. The strength of Masswaweinini was every moment growing fainter. The man of the red feather, small of stature, proved himself very active, but at length he was foiled and thrown to the ground. Immediately his adversary cried out, 'I have thrown you: Wa-ge-me-na,' and in an instant his antagonist had vanished. On looking to the spot where he had fallen he discovered a crooked ear of mondamin, or Indian corn, lying on the ground, with the usual red tassel at the top. While he was gazing at this strange sight, and wondering what it could mean, a voice addressed him from the ground. 'Now,' said the speaking ear, for the voice came from it, 'divest me of my covering, leave nothing to hide my body from your eyes. You must then separate me into parts, pulling off my body from the spine upon which I grow. Throw me into different parts of the plain. Then break my spine and scatter it in small pieces near the edge of the woods, and return to visit the place after one moon.'

"Masswaweinini obeyed these directions, and immediately set out on the return to his lodge. On his way he killed a deer, and on reaching his canoe, he found the boys still asleep. He awoke them and told them to cook his venison, but he carefully concealed from them his adventure. At the expiration of the moon he again, alone, visited his wrestling ground, and to his surprise, found the plain filled with spikes and blades of new grown corn. In this place where he had thrown the pieces of cob, he found pumpkin vines growing in great luxuriance. He concealed this discovery also, carefully from the young lads, and after his return busied himself as usual, in watching the movements of his enemies along the coasts of the islands. This he continued till summer drew near its close. He then directed his canoe to the coast of that part of the island where he had wrestled with the Red Plume, drew up his canoe, bid the lads stay by it, and again visited his wrestling ground. He found the corn in full ear, and the pumpkins of immense size. He plucked ears of corn, and gathered some of the pumpkins, when a voice again addressed him from the corn field. 'Masswaweinini, you have conquered me. Had you not done so your existence would have been forfeited. Victory has crowned your strength, and from henceforth you shall never be in want of my body. It will be nourishment for the human race.' Thus the shaman's people received the gift of corn.

"There were in those days many wonderful things done on the islands. One night while Masswaweinini was laying down, he heard voices speaking, but he still kept his head covered, as if he had not heard them. One voice said, 'This is Masswaweinini, and we must get his heart.' 'In what way can we get it?' said another voice. 'You must put your hand in his mouth,' replied the first voice, 'and draw it out that way.' Masswaweinini still kept quiet, and did not stir. He soon felt the hand of a person thrust in his mouth. When sufficiently far in, he bit off the fingers, and thus escaped danger. The voices then retired, and he was no further molested. On examining the fingers in the morning, what was his surprise to find them long wampum beads, which are held in such high estimation by all Indian tribes. He had slept, as was his custom, in the thick woods. On going out to the open shore at a very early hour, he saw a canoe at a small distance, temporarily drawn up on the beach; on coming closer, he found a man in the bow and another in the stern, with their arms and hands extended in a fixed position. One of them had lost its fingers; it was evidently the man who had attempted to thrust his arm down his throat. They were two Pukwudjinees, or fairies. But on looking closer, they were found to be transformed into statues of stone. The shaman took these stone images on shore, and set them up in the woods.

"Their canoe was one of the most beautiful structures which it is possible to imagine, four fathoms in length, and filled with bags of treasures of every description and of the most exquisite workmanship. These bags were of different weight, according to their contents. He busied himself in quickly carrying them into the woods, together with the canoe, which he concealed in a cave. One of the fairy images then spoke to him and said; 'In this manner, the Ottowa canoes will hereafter be loaded, when they pass along this coast, although your nation are driven away by their cruel enemies the Iroquois.' The day now began to dawn fully, when he returned to his two young companions, who were still asleep. He awoke them, and exultingly bid them to cook, for he had brought abundance of meat and fish, and other viands, the gifts of the fairies.

"After this display of good fortune, he bethought him of his aged father and mother, who were in exile at the Ottawa lake. To wish, and to accomplish his wish, were but the work of an instant with Masswaweinini.

"One night as he lay awake, reflecting on their condition, far away from their native fields, and in exile, he resolved to visit them, and bring them back to behold and to participate in his abundance. To a common traveller, it would be a journey of twenty or thirty days, but Masswaweinini was at the lodge before daylight. He found them asleep, and took them up softly in his arms and flew away with them through the air, and brought them to his camp on the Manatolines, or Spirits Islands. When they awoke, their astonishment was at its highest pitch; and was only equalled by their delight in finding themselves in their son's lodge, in their native country, and surrounded with abundance.

"Masswaweinini went and built them a lodge, near the corn and wrestling plain. He then plucked some ears of corn, and taking some of the pumpkins, brought them to his father and mother. He then told them how he had obtained the precious gift, by wrestling with the spirit in red plumes, and that there was a great abundance of it in his fields. He also told them of the precious canoe of the fairies, loaded with sacks of the most costly and valuable articles. But one thing seemed necessary to complete the happiness of his father, which he observed by seeing him repeatedly at night looking into his smoking pouch. He comprehended his meaning in a moment. 'It is tobacco my father, that you want. You shall also have this comfort in two days.' 'But where?,' replied the old man, 'can you get it away from all supplies, and surrounded by your enemies?' 'My enemies,' he answered, 'shall supply it. I will go over to the Nadowas of the Bear totem, living at Penetanguishine.'

"The old man endeavored to dissuade him from the journey, knowing their blood thirsty character, but in vain. Masswaweinini determined immediately to go. It was now winter weather, the lake was frozen over, but he set out on the ice, and although it is forty leagues, he reached Penetanguishine the same evening. The Nadowas discerned him coming—they were amazed at the swiftness of his motions, and thinking somewhat supernatural, feared him, and invited him to rest in their lodges, but he thanked them saying that he preferred making a fire near the shore. In the evening they visited him, and were anxious to know the object of his journey at so inclement a season. He said it was merely to get some tobacco for his father. They immediately made a contribution of the article and gave it to him. During the night, however, they laid a plot to kill him. Some of the old men rushed into his lodge, their leader crying out to him, 'You are a dead man!' 'No I am not,' said Masswaweinini, 'but you are,' accompanying his words with a blow of his tomahawk, which laid the Nadowa dead at his feet. Another and another came, to supply the place of their fallen comrade, but he dispatched them in like manner, as quickly as they came, until he had killed six. He then took all the tobacco from their smoking pouches. By this time, the day began to dawn, when he set out for his father's lodge, which he reached with incredible speed, and before twilight, spread out his trophies before the old man.

"When spring returned, his cornfield grew up, without planting, or any care on his part, and thus the maize was introduced among his people and their descendants, who have ever been noted, and are at this day, for their fine crops of this grain, and their industry in its cultivation. It is from their custom of trading this article, that this tribe is called Ottowas."

What a magnificent Masswaweinini must have been, and indeed the powers attributed to him are far beyond what an ordinary shaman would possess. Of course this is considered mythology by the contemporary mind—but then myths often have proven to have a foundation in reality. Who can say that there was not, or is not one as powerful as Masswaweinini? One thing can not be denied, the mythological world of the Indian is an excellent complement to his material world, for both show the amazing richness and superb depth of culture that belongs only and forever to the amazing American Indian.

1901 photo shows "Ring of Sacred Cornmeal" ceremony.

Chapter Twelve: The Manabozho Story

Who is Manabozho? He is one of the most unique characters of American Indian mythology. He is not a god, but he has many supernatural, god-like qualities. He was, or is, a serious hero to many Indians, to others the mere mention of his name brings an uproar of laughter, for Manabozho was a bit of a trickster who was often out done by his own tricks.

Manabozho goes by many different spellings which include Wiskendjac and Wenebojo. Manabozho was an agent of Gitchimanitou/The Great Spirit. He was quite active in the creation of the earth. It was Manabozho who obtained the Midaywiwin for his people.

A brief note of explanation. The Midaywiwin or Grand Medicine Society is a sort of secret organization that through the use of herbs and music are able to preform miraculous healings. This society is detailed elsewhere in this book.

Henry R. Schoolcraft, American ethnologist/explorer, prolifically listened to Indian tales and recorded them during a period of the early to mid 1800's. He wrote down hundreds of Indian traditions. During part of this period he served as Commissioner of Indian Affairs at Sault Ste. Marie, Michigan where he married an Indian lady.

He wrote much about Manabozho, who by the way is famously known as Hiawatha and is the focal point of H. W. Longfellows, *The Song of Hiawatha*.

Schoolcraft referred to him as a messenger sent down from the Great Spirit in the form of a wise man and prophet, "but he comes clothed with all the attributes of humanity, as well as the power of performing miraculous deeds. He adapts himself perfectly to their manners, and customs, and ideas.

He is brought up from a child among them. He is made to learn their mode of life. He takes a wife, builds a lodge, hunts and fishes like the rest of them, sings his war songs and medicine songs, goes to war, has his triumphs, has his friends and foes, suffers, wants, hungers, is in dread or joy. His miraculous gifts and powers are always adapted to his situation. His conception was surely on a supernatural note. His ancestry goes something like this: His grandmother is said to have been the daughter of the moon. She had been married only a short time when a rival attracted her to a grape-vine swing at the edge of a lake, and with a single bold shove tossed her into the center of the lake. From this mystical body of water the daughter of the moon fell through the earth. Now she had a daughter, Manabozhol's mother.

At this point we pick up the "supernatural conception." Schoolcraft wrote, "Having a daughter, the fruit of her lunar marriage, she was very careful in instructing her, from early infancy, to beware of the west wind, and never in stooping, to expose herself to its influence. In some unguarded moment this precaution was neglected. In an instant, the gale accomplished its Tarquinic purpose," in other words she was impregnated by the west wind.

Victor Barnouw, in his book, *Wisconsin Chippewa Myths & Tales* (University of Wisconsin/ 1977), relates this story in some detail as it was told to him in 1944 by Tom Badger. He said, "Then one day somebody saw her traveling all alone by herself in the woods. That person seemed to take a liking to her. He even wanted to marry her. He knew what to do. When she was out berrying one nice hot day, when there was no wind, at noon-time, she heard a noise like a gust of wind. She looked around in the direction of the noise and saw a wind coming. When the wind reached her, she couldn't pull her dress down for some time, until the gust of wind went by. She didn't think anything about it because there was no one there to see her."

Fathered by the west wind, Manabozho was of a brood of triplets. They were manitous and their growing up did not take long. Manabozho is said to have killed his brother, the stone.

Very little is known about this manitou's youth. It is known that he lived for a while, during his later youth, on the edge of a great prairie with his grandmother. In fact, as his life's adventures are picked up while at his grandmother's lodge, that place becomes a spring point where his many adventures began. They began simply with little supernatural in them, but progressed into much, much more.

According to the Schoolcraft record, "on this prairie he first saw birds of every kind. He there also saw exhibitions of divine power in the sweeping tempests, in the thunder and lightning, and the various shades of light and darkness, which form never ending observations. Every new sight he beheld in the heavens was a subject of remark; every new animal or bird an object of deep interest; and every sound uttered by the animal creation a new lesson, which he was expected to learn. He often trembled at what he heard and saw. To this scene his grandmother sent him at an early age to watch. The first sound he heard was that of an owl, at which he was greatly terrified, and, quickly descending the tree he had climbed, he ran with alarm to the lodge. 'Noko! Noko!' he cried, 'I heard a manitou!' She laughed at this fear, and asked him what kind of noise it made. He answered, 'It makes a noise like this: Ko-ko-ko-ho!' She told him that he was young and foolish; that what he had heard was only a bird, deriving its name from the noise it made."

At one point he inquired of his grandmother whether or not his father was still alive. She told him that he was and Manabozho set out on a journey to meet his father with every intent of killing him. His grandmother wished for him to wait as the journey to where his father the west wind lived was a long one indeed.

Manabozho, though, was not to be put off. He was now a man and was of giant stature. He was granted by nature great power and strength. His steps were large due to his giant height so that it did not take him long to reach the lodge of the west wind.

The meeting was high atop a mountain, and Ningabiun was very happy to see his son.

They spent several days getting to know each other, but Manabozho was clear and all this time was trying to find what his father's weakness might be. Ningabiun must not have understood the treachery his son was planning for when asked about his weakness he responded to Manabozho, "There is a black stone found in such a place. It is the only thing earthly I am afraid of; for if it should hit me or any part of my body, it would injure me very much."

He inquired the same of his son, that is about his weaknesses. Manabozho stealthfully maneuvered around his inquiring. But with the information gained, Manabozho obtained some of the black rock!

You see, Manabozho was fairly certain that his father had been the cause of his mother's death, this is why he wanted to kill him. Mincing no words the great young manitou asked his father if he had been the cause of his mothers demise, and he responded with the expected affirmative.

There ensued a battle, and I will again turn to Schoolcraft's own telling as he put it so eloquently back in 1856. He said, "Manabozho then took up the rock and struck him. Blow lead to blow, and here commenced an obstinate and furious combat, which continued several days. Fragments of the rock broken off by Manabozhols blows can be seen in various places to this day. This battle commenced on the mountains. The West was forced to give ground. Manabozho drove him across rivers, and over mountains and lakes, and at last he came to the brink of the world.

" 'Hold!' cried he, 'my son, you know my power, and that it is impossible to kill me. Desist, and I will also portion you out with as much power as your brothers. The four quarters of the globe are already occupied; but you can go and do a great deal of good to the people of this earth, which is infested with large serpents, beasts, and monsters, who make great havoc among the inhabitants. Go and do good. You have the power now to do so, and your fame with the beings of this earth will last forever. When you have finished your work, I will have a place provided for you. You will then go and sit with your brother Kabibbooncca in the north.' And by this Manabozho was pacified.

Manabozho was about to undergo another great adventure. Just as Jonah ended up in the belly of the whale, this Indian manitou/prophet was about to become an unsavory mouthful for an unfortunate huge fish swimming in the cold glacial waters of the Great Lakes.

Manabozhol's grandmother was complaining that she had no oils to use on her hair. In order to please her, he built a canoe and rowed out into the middle of the lake so he could catch fish in order to secure more oil for her.

Manabozho kept beckoning the king of fish to come and take his bait by means of a special incantation. A tremendous trout, on hearing him, took hold of the bait. As Manabozho struggled to pull the fish in the canoe almost stood straight on end. Seeing however that this was a large "ugly" trout, he rebuked the fish and it let go of his bait.

The trout was angry with Manabozho, and since he was still chanting, the trout persuaded a monstrous sunfish to take the bait. As Manabozho was pulling this fish in his canoe was being pulled about in swift circles. When he saw that the object of his struggle was a large sunfish, he rebuked it and the sunfish let go of the bait.

Then Manabozhol's bait fell in the water near the king of fish, and hearing that the manitou was still chanting the fish took the bait into his mouth and allowed Manabozho to pull him to the surface. In one gaping mouthful the king of fish swallowed Manabozho and his canoe. When he got his wits about him, he found that he was in the fish's belly.

His thought turned instantly to how he might escape his dilemma. It was his good fortune that he had in the canoe with him, his war club. He hafted the great club and struck out at the fish's heart. The fish became startled and Manabozho could feel it moving swiftly.

Schoolcraft related humorously that the king of fish announced to his comrades that, "I am sick at stomach for having swallowed this dirty fellow, Manabozho." He was about to feel even worse.

The Schoolcraft account of Manabozho in the belly of the king fish states, "Just at this moment he received another severe blow to the heart. Manabozho thought, 'If I am thrown up in the middle of the lake, I shall be drowned, so I must prevent it.' He drew his canoe and placed it across the fish's throat, and just as he had finished the fish commenced vomiting, but to no effect. In this he was aided by a squirrel, who had accompanied him unperceived until that moment. This animal had taken an active part in helping him to place his canoe across the fish's throat."

Manabozhol's attack on the fish's heart was relentless. With many blows to the monster's heart he finally killed the fish. Manabozho knew he had accomplished this end because he could no longer feel the steady motion, but rather could feel the body beating against the shore. But he still needed to get out of the fish.

Manabozho heard birds scratching at the fish's corpse, and he realized that he needed to only bide his time. Soon the birds in their eating broke through, and Manabozho looked at the heads of the gulls as they peered into the hole they had made.

The arrowhead, more importantly, flint knapping was an important part of Indian life. Their arrowheads were made of flint and these in turn were used for hunting and in war. Their knives in early time were made from flint, as were their drills, and a multitude of other tools.

Manabozho is given the credit for learning how to work flint from another manitou and then giving this gift to man. The story says that Manabozho was making arrow shafts for war against the Pearl Feather, but he had no arrow heads.

His grandmother told him that she knew of an old manitou who lived some distance from them, and that he knew how to make the arrow heads. He asked his grandmother to obtain some for him and so she went to the old manitou and returned with many. But Manabozho wanted to learn how to make these points himself. He was forced again to use cunning as his grandmother did not wish to reveal where the old manitou dwelt.

Manabozho implored that she go to get some more, and larger arrow heads. From a distance he followed her and watched from afar how the old manitou made the points so that he could make as many as he would need.

It was also at the old manitou's lodge that he discovered something else, passion. The old manitou's daughter was there, and she was very pretty. He felt his heart pound when he looked at her—but he said nothing. Manabozho returned before his grandmother. She gave him the arrowheads and never suspected a thing.

You can see that as a cultural hero the Indian was able to identify with Manabozho. He had many human characteristics which endeared him to the Indians of the northwoods. Often times his exploits were more humorous. One such story is that of his Grandmother and her "bear" lover, something Manabozho evidently looked down on.

Manabozhol's grandmother sent him far off from her lodge to fast. This would give her time to have her friend in, but Manabozho was suspicious of her. Lets pick up the original Schoolcraft account here.

"Manabozho came near the lodge but called out with a low counterfeited voice, to make it appear that he was distant. She then replied, 'That is far enough.' He had got so near that he could see all that passed in the lodge. He had not long been in his place of concealment, when a paramour in the shape of a bear entered the lodge. He had very long hair. They commenced talking about him, and appeared to be improperly familiar. At that time people lived to be a very great age, and he perceived, from the marked attentions of this visitor, that he did not think a grandmother too old to be pleased with such attentions. He listened to their conversation some time. At last he determined to play the visitor a trick. He took some fire, and when the bear turned his back, touched his long hair. When the animal felt the flames, he jumped out, but the open air only made it burn the fiercer, and he was seen running off in a full blaze."

Now Manabozho was preparing to make war on the Pearl Feather.

This was a great manitou that lived across the waters. He fasted before he ventured forth to battle. He also sung his war songs and beat the drums which is where the modern Indian obtained that tradition. He put a good supply of oil in his canoe, and then fully prepared he set out for battle against the Pearl Feather.

His powers were becoming more developed by this time. He traveled for a full night and a day, but he had only to speak or to will it and the canoe moved forward. He arrived within sight of his first advisory, these were serpents of fire.

The serpents were quite a distance apart and the flames which proceeded from them crossed the path that Manabozho had to take. He began speaking to the serpents as though they were friends, but they were not fooled, they recognized who this was, and they were determined not to let him pass. He cunningly took them by surprise and laughed at them as his canoe slid past them.

There was yet another hazard to navigate before reaching Pearl Feather. This was Pigiu-wagumee or the Pitchwater. This was a section of the lake that was very soft and gummy. Manabozho applied oil to the canoe and then pushed off into the slimey mess. The oil allowed him to slip through the muck with relative ease, though he had to stop frequently to reapply the oil. Manabozho was the first t to ever make it across the Pigiu-wagumee with his life intact.

Schoolcraft tells of the ensuing battle, "He now came in view of land, on which he debarked in safety, and could see the lodge of the Shining Manitou situated high on a hill. He commenced preparing for the fight, putting his arrows and clubs in order, and just at the dawn of day began his attack, yelling and shouting, and crying with triple voices, 'Surround him! Surround him! Run up! Run Up!' making it appear that he had many followers. He advanced crying out, 'It was you that killed my grandfather,' and with this shot his arrows. The combat continued all day. Manabozhol's arrows had no effect, for his antagonist was clothed with pure wampum. He was now reduced to three arrows, and it was only by extraordinary agility that he could escape the blows which the Manitou kept making at him. At that moment a large woodpecker flew past and lit on a tree. 'Manabozho,' he cried, 'your adversary has a vulnerable point; shoot at the lock of hair on the crown of his head.' He shot his first arrow so as only to draw blood from that part. The manitou made one or two unsteady steps, but recovered himself. He began to parley, but, in the act, received a second arrow, which brought him to his knees. But he again recovered. In so doing, however, he exposed his head, and gave his adversary a chance to fire his third arrow, which penetrated deep, and brought him to the ground, a lifeless corpse. Manabozhou uttered his saw-saw-quan, and taking his scalp as trophy, he called the woodpecker to come and receive a reward for his information. He took the blood of the Manitou and rubbed it on the woodpecker's head, the feathers of which are red to this day."

Chapter Thirteen: Manabozho, The Flood, and Points to Ponder

There are many cultural traditions which seem to have a worldwide appeal. The story of a global flood is one example. It is found in almost every culture, and is always depicted as having devastating effects on creation. The Indians of the northeast woodland are no different, they also have a flood tradition in which the earth is destroyed and a new one is created by Manabozho. No matter how much of a buffoon he is sometimes made to look like, in this instance he would appear to have incredible creative powers.

This story is rather lengthy, but quite interesting. Like most Indian allegorical tales, it takes many twists and turns which seem somewhat unnecessary to get to its end. These twists just tend to make the tale more colorful. It is on such a note that the flood story begins.

Manabozho was well known for his expertise as a hunter. One day he was very hungary and he killed a large moose. He found himself in a quandary as to the proper way to eat it. Manabozho thought if he began at the head people would claim he ate it backwards. He determined not to eat it sideways, nor from the back. Finally he decided on a tender portion of the rear section.

Manabozho was about to bite in when there came from a nearby tree a very irritating noise such as is made when branches rub together. Not being able to eat under such circumstance Manabozho commanded the tree to stop. The tree stopped. He was again about to eat when the tree commenced making noise.

Manabozho was now very upset, and even though his stomach burned with hunger, he left the meat to put an end to the noise. He climbed up the tree with swiftness and began tugging and pulling at the noisy limb. As the fates or manitous would have it, Manabozho's arm became caught between the limbs and he was unable to get free.

Now in the woodlands it is the law of the jungle, and you don't pass by unattended food. A pack of wolves took notice of Manabozho and his predicament, then they saw his food. They were no fools. They made away with the entire moose as Manabozho watched on with great remorse and a vengeful spirit spurred on by the fire in his belly.

To late to help satisfy his hunger a heavy wind came up, separated the branches, and he was free. He retired to his lodge in a solemn spirit.

Just for a moment I would like to pick up with the Schoolcraft account of this story as it is pure. He wrote, "Next the old wolf addressed him thus: 'My brother, I am going to separate from you, but I will leave behind me one of the young wolves to be your hunter.' He then departed. In the act Manabozho was disenchanted, and again resumed his mortal shape. He was sorrowful and dejected, but soon resumed his wonted air of cheerfulness. The young wolf who was left with him was a good hunter, and never failed to keep the lodge well supplied with meat. One day he addressed him as follows: 'My grandson I had a dream last night, and it does not portend good. It is of the large lake which lies in that direction. You should be careful never to cross it, even if the ice should appear good. If you should come to it at night weary or hungry, you must make the circuit of it.' Spring commenced, and the snow was melting fast before the rays of the sun, when one evening the wolf came to this lake, weary with the day's chase. He disliked to go so far to make the circuit of it. 'Hwooh!' he exclaimed, 'there can be no great harm in trying the ice, as it appears to be sound.' But he had not got half way across when the ice gave way and he fell in, and was immediately seized by the serpents, who knew it was Manabozho's wolfson, and were thirsting for revenge upon him. Manabozho sat pensively in his lodge."

Manabozho became very concerned as night came on and his wolf son did not return. By the end of the third night his spirit was that of much despair. He realized what had happened though, that his son had not obeyed him and that he died in the lake.

To mourn the loss of the wolf son, Manabozho blackened his face with coal, and fasted for three days until the period of mourning was over. Manabozho then walked to the great lake where he sat upon the shore and cried for his lost son.

A bird alighted by him and inquired as to why Manabozho was there and what the problem was. Manabozho pretended that nothing was wrong and he inquired of the bird as to whether anyone lived in the lake.

The bird is said to have responded that the King of the Serpents lived therein. Stating his own purpose there, and not realizing he was speaking to Manabozho, he told that he was waiting for Manabozho's son to drift ashore. The bird also confirmed that the son had been killed by the serpent.

Manabozho asked him if the serpents ever appeared on land. The bird pointed to a white sandy spot of beach, and informed him that they came there to "bask in the sun." The bird told Manabozho to watch the lake, when it became perfectly still, without so much as a ripple they would appear.

Manabozho attempted to repay the informant not with kindness but by grabbing hold of the bird and trying to wrench its neck off. He got the bird near enough to grab by offering to place on him a white medal. Indeed it was placed and in the scuffle to feathers on the bird's head were mussed—and they ever more stayed this way. The bird became the Kingfisher.

Now like most supernatural beings, Manabozho had the ability to transform himself into other shapes. He went to the sandy beach and transformed himself into the shape of an old oak stump. Not much time had passed and the lake became calm. Multitudes of gigantic serpents came crawling onto the white sands. The Prince of the Serpents was easy to spot for he was perfectly white, all the rest were red and yellow.

Again let's turn to the original Schoolcraft account. At this point it says, "The King of the Serpents said, 'I never saw that black stump standing there before. It may be Manabozho. There is no knowing, but he may be somewhere about here. He has the power of an evil genius, and we should be on our guard against his wiles.' One of the serpents immediately went and twisted himself around it to the top, and pressed it very hard. The greatest pressure happened to be on his throat; he was just about to cry out when the serpent let go. Eight of them went in succession and did the like, but always let go at the moment he was ready to cry out. 'It can not be him. He is too great a weak heart for that.' Then they coiled themselves up in a circle about their Prince. It was not long before they fell asleep."

Making certain that they were all asleep, Manabozho took up his bow and arrows, and with great care he stepped over the serpents till he reached the Prince. With all the strength that his arm could muster, Manabozho pulled the arrow back and shot the pure white Prince in the side!

Manabozho then gave his saw-saw-quan or war cry and ran off as fast as his strong legs would carry him. His loud cry woke the serpents who gave the most horrible wailing cries at the sight of their wounded Prince. Thirsting for the blood of the great manitou Manabozho they set off in pursuit.

Covering miles in a single step Manabozho reached the interior country, but the serpents were also spirits and he could hear their swift approach. He found the very tallest mountain and he climbed the highest tree on its summit. This is when he saw the dreadful sight below him. All the lower lands were now flooded to overflowing. The water was rising rapidly and was gaining on the higher lands. Soon it reached the base of the mountain, and it was not long before the water reached the bottom of the tree. Still the waters did not stop.

The waters continued to rise, soon Manabozho felt his lower body under the water. He commanded the tree to stretch it branches higher, and it did, still the water rose. Again he commanded the tree and once more the branches stretched, but this time the tree told him that it could stretch no more.

Finally the waters began to recede and Manabozho felt a great relief, but the waters were still deep and had ruined the earth. Manabozho saw a loon swimming about and he commanded him to dive down in the waters, and to bring up some dirt so that he could create a new earth. The bird did as he was commanded but the depth overcame him and he floated to the surface dead.

Then Manabozho spotted a muskrat and commanded him to do the same. The muskrat dove down but floated up to the surface dead. Manabozho lifted the body and breathed into its nostrils and once more the creature lived. He was commanded to try again, and he did. The muskrat again came to the surface dead. This time, though it clutched a little earth. Manabozho took the earth, the muskrat, and the loon, and he created from them a new earth.

Manabozho went about surveying the new creation and he heard a voice singing. He found a female spirit disguised as an old woman and she was singing lamentations. Manabozho asked her what was wrong.

She explained to him that her son the Prince of Serpents had been shot by Manabozho in revenge for the loss of his son, and that now the earth had overflowed and been created anew. Not realizing who she was speaking with, she told him that she had brought her son to the new world so that he might destroy its inhabitants and thus have his revenge on Manabozho. She also explained that she was searching for herbs to cure her son.

Manabozho was not to be defeated, so he put the female spirit to death, took off her skin and put it on self for a disguise. On his way to her lodge, he was met by a spirit who told him to hurry for the Prince was much worse.

At the lodge was the most horrible sight to his eyes, they had skinned his wolf son and were using his skin as door to the lodge. He was this time to revenge his son totally!

Manabozho sat down by the door of the lodge and he began crying and lamenting just as the old lady had done. He rose and signing the songs of the old woman he approached the Prince. No one suspected that he was an imposter.

He saw that his arrow remained in place in the serpent, and that it had sunk about half way in. He acted as though he was about to pull the arrow out but instead he gave it a sudden thrust and killed the prince! The shear power of his movement burst the skin of the old woman. Manabozho busted through the door and ran out with the serpents in hot pursuit. Manabozho then transformed himself into a wolf and attained great speed aided by his father the West Wind.

Thus is the account of the great flood as told in the northeast lands. But Manabozho had many other adventures, and they were favorites for being told around the campfire. Although this particular flood account is told with much abstraction, threads of a biblical account, especially the theme of good over evil are intricately woven through the story line.

Manabozho became rather disgusted with the arrival of the white man and decided he would travel west to live. In the book, *Bloodstoppers & Bearwalkers,* Richard M. Dorson related the story of this westward migration as told to him by Mike Sogwin-

Mr. Sogwin said, "So Manabozho goes West, says he is finished, is going to a rock formation, because the white man is coming. He says he will always be glad to see the younger generation though. About four or five hundred years ago the last bunch went out. He asked them what they wanted. Some asked to live one, two, three, or four hundred years; others asked for medicine and things like that. The old people had told the boys before they went out, 'Don't ask for more than four lives— four hundred years.' But some of the boys made up their minds they wanted to live the rest of the world. So Manabozho changed them into black granite— the only rock that never rots.

"In my mothers time one guy went out and asked for four hundred years. On the way back with the party a grizzly bear tore him all into pieces. The rest saw that happen and ran away while the bear was destroying their comrade. When they went back they saw him all together again, but scarred up. Manabozho had brought him together again to finish his four hundred years. In the village he never wore any clothes, just a little diaper, so everyone could see the scars. Oh, he was terribly marked. My mother saw him, so it must have been so. That was the last bunch that ever went out from around here."

Brad and Sherry Steiger in their fascinating book, *Mystical Legends of the Shamans* (Inner Light Publications/1991) tell a little more about Manabozhols origins.

They said, "Legend tells of a great spirit being from the stars who visited earth and who became enamored of an Indian maiden. Their first born son was Mannabozho, the friend of the human race." They go on to tell, "The power symbol of Manabozho is depicted with horn attached to a circular helmet that suggests an unbroken oneness with all humankind."

Many more tales could be told about the exploits of Manabozho, but he is just one of many legendary characters of the great northeast woodland culture, so it is time to move on.

Chapter Fourteen: The Origins of Man

There are multitudes of accounts pertaining to the origin of man. Some theories have us evolving from subspecies, others say we were deposited here by extraterrestrials. Because I enjoy feeling special, my favorite is the scriptural account where a loving creator fashions man from the earth into his own image, then breathed life into the nostrils of mankind. This sort of makes me feel unique.

The Indian cultures of the northeast have many legends pertaining to the creation of man. These tales are filled with rich color. Three such stories stand above all the rest.

First is a story called, "Gaw-be-naw, The First Man." Created by Gitchi-Manitou/The Great Spirit, Gaw-be-naw, was said to be the original man. He was made to rule over all the land and the seas. He helped Gitchi-Manitou name all the animals. He taught the people how to plant seeds and cultivate gardens, as well as to hunt, fish, build wigwams, make canoes, how to count, and how to make clothes from the skins of animals. Gaw-be-naw was also considered to have been a prophet, philosopher, and a leader of great natural ability.

In the now rather obscure book, *The Crooked Tree,* author John C. Wright spoke of Gaw-be-naw. He said, "The snowshoe, bow and arrow, stone tomahawk, pe-no-gawn or warm winter house, and all such devices and inventions were said to have been introduced by Gaw-be-naw. Volumes could be written of his genius and prowess. No task was too difficult for him to accomplish, no obstacle to great for this wonderful man to overcome. He was greatly beloved by the Great Spirit who favored him in all things."

How long this first man lived no one knows. It is just said that he was of a great age. During the early part of his reign as chief all of his people were happy. It is as though he sustained their needs; they were happy, there were no wars, and there was no dissension or any kind of trouble.

As the great chief Gaw-be-naw grew into the gray years his sustaining powers seem to have failed. Drought and famine spread over the face of the earth in his later days.

The crumbling of his "empire" was said to have been sent by the Great Spirit as a punishment. Gaw-be-naw had become quite bold, and he foolishly thought himself to be all powerful and responsible for the growth of the crops. He failed to give thanks or to consult the Great Spirit.

It was only after the drought and famine had come that Gaw-be-naw began to fast and pray for rain so that the people would survive. But no rain came. Gaw-be-naw announced that he would travel to the land of Gitchi-Manitou and would intercede for his people. Here is another of many examples where early people were able, seemingly at will, to leave the earth sojourn into the land of the spirits. This is a theme that holds through much of Indian mythology.

Let's again go to John C. Wright's accountMr. Wright said that, "He traveled many, many days, and at last came to the dwelling place of the Ruler of Creation, who said:

"'Gaw-be-naw, my child, you have been very disobedient. I have made you the ruler over the land and sea; but I alone have power over the sun and moon, to make the crops grow and the trees to bear fruit. But though you have displeased me I will have compassion on my people. Hereafter Ah-nim-o-kee will sit at my side and when rain is needed he will beat upon his drum. When he pounds with his drumstick, thunder will roll over the Earth; when he opens his eyes, lightning will flash and the people will rejoice, for it will be a sign that I will send water to moisten the ground so that grain will grow in abundance and famine will no longer occur.'"

Now far to the west, past the rivers, the trees and the mountains, beyond even the seas, there is an old warrior who sits with his back towards the earth. This is Ah-nim-o-kee or the Thunderer. When he is signaled by the Great Spirit, Ah-nim-o-kee beats his drum and flashes his eyes, bringing rain to revive and to nourish the earth and its people.

In Indian mythology animals play various power roles. In this next story, "Mich-I-bou and the First Man," the rabbit plays an important creative role.

The Great Hare, who is named Mich-i-bou, sat upon the surface of the waters with all the various creatures he had made. Mich-i-bou had four legs, and two served the purpose of arms. His creations were all different, and some were quite unusual to behold. There were those that had but one leg, others had as many as twenty. Others had arms and no legs. Everything varied including the numbers of eyes and noses. The most unusual of all the creatures in appearance was Mich-i-bou himself.

In this story the creator had a wife, and it is said that his wife was as odd looking as was he. They had many children, and on the day that she was to deliver his one thousandth child she had a vision. She was shown that this unborn child would need a place which was solid to dwell. Mich-I-bou was perplexed by this. He decided to create such a place, and to do this he dove beneath the waters and brought to the surface a grain of sand.

In particular Mich-i-bouls next act showed the unlimited creative power which he was alleged to have possessed. He took the grain of sand and blew on it, and kept on blowing on it until an island was formed. It was set a float and upon its dry shores the first man was born. His name was A-to-a-can which meant the Great Father. A-to-a-can was gigantic and he soared in height above even the most tall trees.

A-to-a-can was quite alone though and he was of somber spirit. The spring brought bright and beautiful wild flowers, trees heavy burdened with luscious fruits, there were bushes clustered with large ripe berries, but none of this made him happy.

A-to-a-can put clay upon his head and called out with loneliness, "Os-se-maw Father, I am alone. You have created a beautiful place, please give to me someone with which to share it."

By this time Mich-i-bou was no longer dwelling on the earth but in the heavens where he watched over his creation. Here we learn of the possible concept of angels, but certainly of spiritual beings and the concept that they could come down to earth to indwell with man.

At this point, Mich-i-bou looked around himself at the people with him in the air, and he saw a beautiful woman whose name was A-ta-hen-sic. She was bright and shinning like the sun, and it is told around the campfire that she was as beautiful as the moon.

To A-ta-hen-sic's delight, Mich-i-bou offered her a trip to the earth. She was also more than delighted to share her life with the handsome giant who dwelt below. Mich-i-bou made a rope from the sinew and tendons of animals, and he lowered A-ta-hen-sic down to the lodge of his beloved son.

A-to-a-can was now more at peace with life. He went out to hunt and was comforted knowing that his lovely wife would be there on his return. As the course of time progressed a boy and girl were born to the couple. In turn as they grew up they moved away from the parents and built a new lodge and the earth slowly became populated.

Mich-i-bou was not pleased with the slowness with which the earth was being populated. He taught his son and grandson another method. They were told that when any animal died they were to skin it and burn the skin. Then they would take a drop of their own blood and place it on the remains of the dead animal. This then was covered with leaves. With the passing of four days they were instructed to remove the leaves and they would find an infant that would cry with delight at now being a human. Having thus accomplished this purpose, Mich-i-bou returned to the sky and was never seen again.

Following these instructions the earth was soon populated with new people recreated from the dead remains of four footed animals.

Many Indians of the northeast feel that people today still bear the marks of this creation. For example those with red skin like the moose are brave and strong, those who are crafty and fast come from the red fox. Most often in mythology the white skinned people are represented as evil and weak. Here we find that it is believed that the white skins who are cowardly are made from rabbits.

Lastly we will look at a legend which was told by a full blooded Indian who lived at Manistque, Michigan at the turn of the century. His name was Cornstalk, and he was so old that he is said to remember the War of 1812!

Though it has nothing to do with the origin of man, the following is added to show his strength of character. On one bitter cold day in the winter time a tree fell on Cornstalks leg and pinned him to the ground so that he could not get up. He knew that if he remained there he would freeze to death. He reached into his pocket, withdrew his knife then cut his leg off and crept home on his hands and knees!

Of particular interest here though is a story that old Cornstalk told called, "Why The Pine Trees Weep."

This story was originally published in *The Crooked Tree,* by John C. Wright back in 1915. The story explains why drops of water like rain sometimes fall from pine trees.

"Mongo, according to Cornstalk, was the first man that inhabited the earth. He came from the land of the rising sun and made his home along the streams of the north and the shores of the Great Lakes. Although fish and game were plentiful, Mongo was dissatisfied and lonesome, for he had no companion to share his joys. The Great Spirit saw that his heart was sad, and one night as Mongo sat in front of his wigwam warming himself by a huge campfire, he was suddenly startled by a bright light in the heavens; and on looking up he saw a meteor swiftly descend to the earth, leaving a train of flames in its wake. The bright ball fell only a short distance from where he was seated and as it fell it burst into many pieces and a beautiful woman stood before him.

"Mongo was frightened and would have fled, but the woman held out her hand and beckoned him to come. Mongo's fear suddenly left him and a new, strange passion, that of love, took its place and filled his soul. He lead Wasaqua, which name means, the new born light, to his wigwam on the banks of the roaring Escanaba, where for many moons they lived together happily and several children were born to them to bless their union. But one day Mongo became sick, and although Wasaqua nursed him with all a woman's tender care, he sank rapidly and before many days died.

"Wasaqua was inconsolable. She lay upon Mongo's grave and wept and dampened the earth with her tears. She refused food and would not be comforted. The birds and the beasts brought her many tender morsels, but she put them aside.

"At night bears and wolves laid down by her side to keep her warm; but her grief kept increasing until nature could stand it no longer and she fell into the sleep that knows no waking. She was laid in the grave by the side of her husband at the end of the day: and the whippoorwill's voice was hushed and the howl of the wolf echoed not through the forest, so great was the grief of all living creatures.

"But before the sun shone upon the grave again, a great pine, like a solitary, watchful sentinel, stood at the head of the mound where the first man and woman were returned to the earth to mix forever with the elements.

"The pine was the first of its kind among the monarchs of the forest and night and day it wept and sang sweet, sad requiem over the lonely mound. And to this day the pine trees weep and moan and sigh for the first born of the earth."

And so was the coming of man into the world, and his exit from the world according to the traditions of the northeast woodland cultures.

Chapter Fifteen: In The Heavens and On The Earth

In Indian mythology there are many cases where spiritual beings come down from the sky places to dwell with humans. Often times man is also able to ascend into the sky to the land where the spirits dwell, without having to die first. There are even fascinating accounts where humans have gone into the sky and have been transformed into celestial objects.

Most say these are just legends and have no basis in reality. I ask why? Who knows what transpired in the dim past? Perhaps some of these shaman's legends are not as far fetched as our anglo-culture minds might have us believe. Lets take for instance the story of the North Star.

It is told in the course of this story, that not all Indians believed in marriage. When a brave would not marry he was said to belong to the Two Cousins.

But who are the Two Cousins? Legend has it that many years ago their were two brave warriors that became very enamored of each other. They were so close that they made a vow to never separate.

They lived in the lodge of their grandmother who preformed certain responsibilities of the wife, such as fixing their meals and dressing, their game. Up in years though the grandmother got tired of this extra work that should not have been her burden to carry. One day while the companions were out hunting she invited to her lodge two beautiful maidens.

When the young men returned playfully laughing, the grandmother confronted them and said something to the effect of, "My children I am growing old and weak. The work of dressing all the game you bring is too great a task; therefore I have asked these two beautiful women to be your wives, and they have consented to do this."

They were dumb struck and did not know how to respond. In the beginning they went about their daily affairs and made no attempt to be husbands to these maidens. But the maidens were persistent and remained pleasant to their unattending husbands. At last the younger of the two men fell in love with his wife.

When the two went out to hunt the younger could hardly kill anything for his mind kept returning to his new sweetheart. He obtained only three bear skins this day as opposed to the 20 the older brave took. The older knew that something was wrong, and the younger brave told him of the intentions of his heart.

In anger the older brave told him that this being the case he would never again set his foot in their direction. The younger man tried to change his mind but this was to no avail, and the older brave started off toward the north.

He turned and told his friend, "Although I leave you, remember that if you are ever alone at

The Sacred "Ghost Dance."

night and need a friend, you will see me up there in the northern heavens. If you ever get lost in the forest or at any time cannot find your way in the darkness, I will always be there to guide your footsteps."

The older brave was true to his words, and after speaking began to walk up into the Sky where he assumed the form of a star. He is there to this day, the bright north star, chasing the bear just as he did in the old days when he hunted the woods of the woods of the northeast woodland.

The young brave was totally distraught over the loss of his friend, and he was wasting away before he even reached home. He became only a shadow. Every since he has roamed the hills and valleys hiding away from any humans who might have passed by. His name became Bah-swa-way or Echo, and his time is spent mocking and laughing at everyone.

The two maidens waited and waited for their lovers to return. Filled with disappointment, the young maidens rose into the sky where they could better watch for the braves return. They became the Morning and the Evening star.

Impossible you say? We all know that love, or lack thereof can do unusual things to people, in this case it transformed them into stars.

One of the best stories in this category has its origins is the Shawnee traditions. It is the story of Waupee and The Star Family, subtitled, "The Celestial Sisters." This story is another that we owe a debt of thanks to Henry R. Schoolcraft for. In this story, you will find many references which will lead the mind to "extra terrestrial" visitation. Cutting through the symbolism, this just might be the case.

Waupee was also known as the White Hawk. He lived in a very remote part of the forest where wild game was plentiful. He was successful every day in the hunt and always returned with lots of game to show for his effort. Among his tribe he was the most respected hunter.

White Hawk was gifted with a tall, handsome, manly form—the bright fires of youth flared in his eyes. He was afraid of nothing, not even the densest and most gloomy of forest.

One day Waupee penetrated deep into the forest. He went way beyond any point where man had before travelled. Finally he saw light through the dense pine trees and discovered that he was on the edge of a wide plain that abounded with colorful wild flowers and rich green grass.

As he walked on, White Hawk happened upon a most curious spot. There was a large ring worn in the sod as though it had been made by constant foot travel. He was excited to also discover a path leading to and from the circle. But he could find no trace of a foot step, not a broken twig or crushed leaf. Being quite curious Waupee took up a post and was of a mind to wait and see what purpose this circle served.

Before long there came through the sweet woodland air the sound of music. He looked up, for that is the direction from which the music came, and descending was a small object.

The object moved with great speed. At first it looked like a small speck, but then was discernible as a basket. As the heavenly basket moved closer the music became louder and much more pleasing to him.

The basket was filled with twelve sisters who were all possessed of beautiful form. When the basket was securely on the ground the sisters jumped out, and around the magic ring they began to dance performing a curious act as they did. Waupee observed that they were striking a shining ball as his people would strike a drum.

From his secure hiding place White Hawk drank in their graceful forms and exotic motions. They all pleased him and made his heart race with passion, but the most desirable to him was the youngest.

He was unable to restrain himself longer, he wanted her to be his. He rushed out from his hiding place and attempted to take hold of her. But the celestial sisters were swift. The instant they saw him they leaped back into the basket and once more ascended to their home in the sky.

Waupee was upset by his ill fortune and he stared at the heavens until they were out of sight. He returned to his lodge in lonely despair, certain that he would not see them again.

Now you need to remember that the people of these early times were possessed of special powers. They were able to seemingly transform themselves at will into other shapes. White Hawk was going to attempt to put this ability to his use.

He returned to the prairie on the following day, and in an effort to deceive the sisters he changed his shape into that of an opossum. His wait was not a

97

long one as before long he heard the lovely music and the heavenly basket once more descended.

The sisters once again began their dancing, and to Waupee they seemed even more lovely than on the previous day. Slowly under cover of his disguise, White Hawk crept towards the magic ring. Once more the sisters were startled by him and sprung into the basket. This time the basket rose a only a little way, they observed him for a moment and then as the sisters began to chant the basket continued rising.

White Hawk once more returned to his lodge feeling very down hearted. The night was a long one for him, but the next day he decided to return once again to the magic circle. This time he gave a little more thought as to how to go undetected by the sisters. Nearby the magic circle was a stump that was inhabited by mice. Waupee observed their form, and being so small thought they would not alarm the sisters, so he took the form of a mouse. He moved the stump near to the ring. Again the sisters came down and they resumed their dancing.

"See!" said the youngest sister, "There was no stump here before." She was frightened by this and ran back towards the celestial basket. But the rest made fun, they struck the stump and the mice came running out, Waupee right along with them. The sisters killed all the mice except Waupee and he was pursued by the object of his desire, the younger sister. Just as she rose her stick to deal a killing blow to the little rodent, White Hawk again assumed his human form. He caught hold of his prize and held her firmly in his strong arms. The remaining eleven sisters again entered the basket with great swiftness and were gone.

Waupee tried all he could think of to please his bride and to win her heart and love. She missed her sisters and he would gently wipe the tears away with his strong hand. He would entertain her with daring stories of his hunts, and then would tell her of the many delights life on earth held. He picked their path carefully and lead her to his lodge. When she entered it his heart leapt with joy, and he was made one of the happiest of men by his new bride.

Winter and summer came and left, and their joy was increased as they were gifted with a handsome son.

But there could be no denying that she was a daughter of the stars, and the charms of life on earth began to dissatisfy her. She longed to once more visit her father. She was deceitful in relation to her husband as she withheld from him her feelings and plotted to return to the stars. She remembered well the incantation she and her sisters had used. While White Hawk was busied with the hunt, his lovely wife used the time to construct another basket. As this was going on she would also spend time collecting specimens of rare and wonderful things of the earth with which to gift her father.

One day while Waupee was out on the hunt, she took their son and the basket and went to the magic circle. When she placed him in the basket she also got in and then began singing and the basket in turn rose. Carried by the wind her voice reached her husband's ears. He ran instantly with great fear to the prairie for he knew what was taking place behind his back. He reached the ring but was powerless to do anything. All he could do was watch the basket rise with his wife and child. His heart sunk and White Hawk felt as though his life had now ended.

The winter which followed was a long one indeed. He bewailed his loss even through the following summer. He longed for his wife, but even more for his young son.

Now his wife had reached her home in the stars. She was so content with life in the sky that she was near to forgetting that she had an earthbound husband. She was reminded of this though by the son, who as he grew up longed to see the place where he was born and to meet his father.

One day her father commanded her to go and take the child to earth to meet his father, adding that she should ask him to come up into the sky to live with them. The father also asked that she ask her husband to bring with them one of each type of animal he killed in his hunting.

She took the boy and returned to earth uncertain what reaction she would receive after her horrible misdeed. Waupee was near the magic circle when he heard her voice and saw the basket coming down from the sky. His heart beat rapidly with anticipation as he gazed upon her form and that of their son. Soon they were all embraced in each others arms.

When he heard the request of her father he began to hunt with great earnest. He spent days and nights in search of the most beautiful birds and animals to please her father. Oddly, though, Waupee only preserved a tail, foot or wing of each in order to identify them. When all was prepared the family entered the basket and ascended to the sky.

There was great joy when they arrived at the plain of stars. The Star Chief had prepared a feast and all the people were invited to it. As all assembled the Chief announced that they could all partake of gifts such as they liked best. There immediately arose a great confusion amongst the people. Some had chosen a wing, or a foot, or a tail. Those who had selected tails or claws were right away turned into animals. The rest took the form of birds and they flew away. Waupee, his wife and their son selected a white hawk's feather, and each became a white hawk. The Star Chief also selected a white hawk feather and delighted with his new found vitality, the chief spread out his wings and followed his family as they descended to earth. Their descendants are among us yet today.

I read a story like this of the Celestial Sisters, and I have to wonder how anyone could doubt that the Shawnee at least, had some knowledge that there were in actual, literal fact, beings living in the sky—perhaps on other planets. The ending is rather shrouded in symbolism but that should not take away from the message which might lie in such a tale.

A story called, "The Origin of the Medicine Lodge" is yet another which draws together the heaven and the earth. It is worth taking a look at.

According to this tale, the heaven and the earth were at one time connected by a great vine down which spiritual beings could climb to reach earth. This was early in the history of man on earth, but at this point in time, the Great Spirit had decreed that no mortals could ascend into the heavens.

It so happened though that one young man was taken quite ill. He was so sick that he was delirious, and in this state he climbed far up the vine, out of sight. His mother was so saddened by the loss of her son in this manner that she embarked up the vine in an attempt to find him. The effort was useless as her added weight to the vine caused it to snap and she and the boy both feel back to earth in a heap.

Gitchi-Manitou, the Great Spirit, was very angry with the people over this. He made a decree, "Sickness and disease will prevail amongst you, and instead of living on forever you will die when you grow old. There is only one thing for you to do. Remember that everything that grows has some value, nothing was made in vain. Therefore you will gather roots and herbs and compound medicines and these will help you when in distress."

On this note, according to this legend, was the Medicine Lodge of the Midaywiwin established between the Great Spirit and man. Other legends state very clearly that Manabozho was the one who helped man establish the Midaywiwin—he was a messenger of the Great Spirit, and was himself a manitou.

In the Straits of Mackinaw lying in Lake Huron near the tip of Michigan's lower peninsula, is Mackinaw Island. Today Mackinaw is an expensive tourist trap. On a recent visit to the island I was even charged for a glass of water. To the Indians of the northeast woodland Mackinaw was and is a sacred place. It is the Great Turtle, the earthly home of Gitchi-Manitou/The Great Spirit.

Many strange and fearsome beasts have dwelt upon this island's mystic shoreline. Many of them were spirits, sorcerers and shamans. These legends will be touched upon later. There were also connections between this island, its people, and the sky dwellers. Mackinaw the Great Turtle is possessed of many unusual geographical features, one is Arch Rock, and this next legend of the sky people touching humanity is about, "The Great Arch Rock."

This unusual rock architecture is revered by the Indians, and is considered the bridge over which the souls of deceased could find a resting place in the many caves which punctuate the island.

A band of Chippewa were dwelling along the shoreline of Lake Huron. One lodge stood out amongst them as the finest. For its door hung a beautifully prepared moose hide. This is where the chief lived with his daughter named, She-who-walks-like-the-mist. She was much admired by the young braves of the tribe. The daughter was brilliant with her craft work of quills and dyed moose hair. She did not pay much attention to her admirers though.

Mist Woman had very long days with no help in her work, for her mother had passed away. She knew in her heart of hearts that some day she would find a fine young brave from another clan, marry him and give to him many children.

As she came to courting age many of the young men brought gifts to her father's lodge, and she received them repaying the amorous young men with wild rice, which she herself had collected. She seemed to enjoy the attention that was being shown to her.

One day, however, she stopped acknowledging the attentions of the braves. Rather, gifting them with her lovely smile, she would sit with eyes down cast. Her father became distraught and angary with Mist Woman as he saw her closing more into herself.

The Chief inquired of her why she was treating the young braves with a cold heart. In fact, he even wondered if some sorcerer had cast an evil spell upon her.

Mist Woman was defiant and would give her father no answer.

She was warned by him that she could dwell in his lodge only so long, and that soon she would have to select a husband. Defying her father she still remained silent.

Her silence made the Chief very angary, and he stood with a heavy stick he had retrieved from the ground. The Chief told Mist Woman, "Never have I raised my hand against you, but I will if you do not obey my wishes in this matter."

Seeing the anger and hurt she was causing her father, Mist Woman at last spoke. She confirmed that she was under a spell, but not that of a sorcerer, and she proceeded to explain.

"I will tell you father so that you may know my heart and not be worried. Many times when I go alone to gather the wild rice it is quite late, and when I return the star path of the dead is already in the sky. Two nights ago as I paddled to the eastern shore, a brave that is very handsome came to me.

"Father, his clothing was the most wonderful I have ever seen. It was made of pure white deer skin, and it was covered with designs such as my eyes have never before seen. But even more beautiful was his robe, for that robe was of shinning light. I tried to paddle safely home, but it was as if I had no will and my canoe drifted to him and he spoke to me. He called me Lovely One, and he said that he had watched me in our village and had longed that I could be his forever. He told me that in his home in the sky he is the son of a chief, son of the Evening Star. This is why, my father, that I felt I could not tell you about my love. He told me that he would watch as the young men came to this lodge and that he became sick with despair. He said his father came to his bed of bird feathers and that he told his father of my beauty. The Star Chief was understanding and granted him permission to come to the earth and ask me to join him in his home in the stars. I told him that I would marry no one but him!"

Her father became even more furious and shouted that he forbid the marriage to take place. He caught he by the arm and shoved Mist Woman out the door and down to the lake shore. He placed her in the bow of his canoe with no respect to her feelings and then with massive strokes paddled out to Island of the Turtle Spirits, Mackinaw. He had in the canoe a rope made of deer sinew, and he cast a noose about his daughter, and dragged her to a great rock standing tall above the beach. He tied her hand and foot and defiantly informed her that she would never see her lover again. He told her that the rock would be her home until she decided to be a faithful daughter once more.

Mist Woman remained there proudly and did not cry out for help, not even when the hot sun beat upon her or the rain slashed at her. Her tears flowed down upon the rock and bespoke of her down trodden heart.

Her tears gradually wore away the stone until an arch appeared beneath her and she was left on a high bridge. In the dark of night the evening star appeared, and her handsome brave rode down the star beams. He picked Mist Woman up in his arms and carried her back up the star beams into the land of the star people, where they lived happily.

In this account we see a different element. Here rather than being held sacred and welcomed, the star dwellers or extraterrestrials were looked down upon, and an impending mixed marriage was scorned by her father. Why was this spirit/human marriage frowned on? An interesting comparison can be drawn between this attitude and the attitude in the Old Testament when because of such inter-marriage God became very angry with the resulting evil and the world was destroyed by the flood. It is interesting nonetheless that the sky people have been such an influence on so many cultures through out human history, but none of the accounts seem so graphic to me as those of the American Indian.

Chapter Sixteen: Fearsome Manitous and Frightening Creatures

The northeast woodlands, and the mythology of the northeast have been the habitation for many fearsome beasts—both real and imagined.

For example, giants are said to have been abundant in one form or another in past times. Here in my own home county, when farming came to be a mainstay occupation in the mid 1870's, skeletons were excavated by the farmers. These were not preserved, nor were there specific measurements given, just that they were very gigantic in proportion. Some of the giants were even believed to be cannibals.

One legend about the giants is titled, "The Crack". It is said that the islands of northern Lake Huron were once inhabited by a tribe of very red skinned giants. When the giants died they did not go up the trail of souls but instead became spirits in waiting or demons who wandered about. The disposition of the spirit was up to the divine judgement of Gitchi-Manitou, the Great Spirit.

The spirits who were in waiting often took the form of conical rocks, boulders or pinnacles. The wandering demons, though, were given the form of men who were truly heartless and totally barbaric in their nature.

Though its location is not now known, there was reported a field of several acres which were property of the United States. Splitting this field from one end to the next is a large crack. It has been described as a, "Deep and mysterious chasm. A frightful place, full of dark shadows and mournful echoings, which no man ever penetrated successfully, its steep sides offering no foothold, and of the unwary ones who have stumbled headlong into the crack, none have returned to tell of its mysteries."

Indians and whites were both frightened of this place. They would not take game that was shot in its vicinity. The site was avoided at all cost, and even if starving the Indians would refuse to eat food from there.

The crack is believed to be possessed by the spirit of one of the demon giants. The legends says, "The demon was so foolish as to wish to penetrate the Under Land where the Spirits of the Dead held sway. This of course was not permitted, and the giant's fingers were never released from the fissure in the rock where he clung, and from which those who have good eyes declare he may still be seen hanging above the abyss.

"Five immense fingers, the knuckles, back of the hand, and wrist are still distinctly visible beneath the scales of limestone with which the ages have covered them."

It is commonly held as truth that the giant's curse befalls those who walk on the clinging digits, even if done by accident. It has been reported that sickness, blindness, loss of wealth, and misfortune in love are among the circumstances encountered after the curse has been set. Though he is still under punishment of the Great Spirit, the demon giant still has malignant powers and delights in using them.

The giant of the crevice is not a match for the wickedness of the wen-di-goes who are cannibal giants. The wen-di-goes, along with their partners in crime, the red gee-bis—are said to have dwelled on Mackinaw Island. Again, Mackinaw was at one time the earthly abode of the Great Spirit. By the way, the

Medicine man uses prayer stick to foretell events.

red gee-bis are said to be cannibal sorcerers.

The following story takes place on Mackinaw Island, and in it we will learn a little of how nasty these creatures were able to be. The story, called "The Devil's Kitchen," is told in many volumes with considerable variation. That I am about to tell you is compiled from the various sources.

Aikie-wai-sie was blind and very old. His people were breaking camp to move inland for the winter. They tore down their wigwams, took up their fire poles, and they dug their sacred items from the ground. But the old man was left behind to die of starvation, it was a hard lot for him, but quite by accident his granddaughter had also been left behind. Her name was Willow Wand. This added greatly to his discontent as he was beyond the age of being able to care for her needs.

Then Willow Wand was very angry when she learned of the treatment which had been dolled out to her grandfather and herself. There was no hope of escaping from the island as all the boats had been removed. But though there was good reason to be, Willow Wand was not afraid. She set out with a plan of signaling fishermen who came close by to put out their nets. There was a white cliff, and from the cliff she hung a red blanket hoping to catch someone's attention.

Willow Wand was in love with a handsome young brave named Kewe-naw. They were pledged to be married. One day Kewe-naw had thrown a white doe by the door of her lodge, by its acceptance her approval of him as a husband was shown. Soon after the acceptance of the proposal Kewe-naw had to leave the island, and the tribe had broken up before his return. Willow Wand knew he would be furious and would seek them out. Being at the fishing grounds to the north, Kewe-naw might not hear of the dilemma for months; by then their fate might be sealed.

When the red blanket had been properly secured, Willow Wand lead her grandfather along a ledge in the side of the cliff. From this observation point they would watch for the fishermen.

Ailie-wai-sie had a dreadful secret fear which he did not share with Willow Wand. He worried that the men of his tribe might become very hungary, even to the point of returning to the island and making a feast of him. He wondered what cruel fate might then await Willow Wand.

The ledge which they sought out was near the cave of the dreadful Red Geebis who feed on nothing but human flesh. The grandfather reasoned that by way of being near the Red Geebis, he and Willow Wand would be safe from human assault.

Behind the stranded couple slept a great female bear. Willow Wand considered this an opportunity to gain food for her and Aikiewai-sie. He was, however, against killing the bear and commanded that she be left alone to continue her sleep. Obeying Aikie-waisie, Willow Wand cast herself upon a crude bed made of piled leaves and tried hard to forget the pangs of hunger in her stomach, and the pains of desertion in her heart.

Provisions were scanty indeed. As their early meal they had but a bit of dry corn and some pounded pemmican. To take her mind off their dire straits Aikie-wai-sie told Willow Wand stories of the great Turtle god, and of his bright and grand green robes. He told her also of the caves where the giant fairies dwell until it is time for them to be called upon to dance the last dance.

The grandfather told Willow Wand a story of how he had once been under the influence of witchcraft and had been transformed into a deer. Only by agreeing to his blindness was he able to once again become human. Finally after the telling of many stories Willow Wand passed into that mystical world of dreams.

Night fell and the dark shadows crept over the world. There was no moon nor stars in the dark sky. There was a flaming red light coming from the Devil's Cave. The eerie red glow reflected off Aikie-wai-sie's white hair and the flushed face of Willow Wand, who even in her sleep called out for water.

Spurred by the girl's pitiful sleep talk of thirst, Aikie-wai-sie's memory flitted back in time to the moments just before Willow Wand's mother died. She had confessed to him a magical gift that her lovely little daughter had inherited from her father the Willow.

With merely a command from the girl, springs of pure water would begin to flow wherever she directed. Willow Wand's mother said that this power would bring the girl great fame as a prophet and a healer—but that the knowledge must remain hidden until the daughter of Whispering Birch was wise, and Aikie-waisie wondered if it was not the appropriate time for him to make the revelation. As is the custom of the Indian people, Willow Wand had to go through the vision quest before becoming an adult, so the grandfather had determined to not yet reveal the secret.

The girl suffered greatly from hunger and thirst. After seven days, fearing that she might die, Aikie-wai-sie, not caring that he might be caught by the Red Geebis, left the security of the ledge to secure water for Willow Wand. Upon his return the girl was still crying out in delirium for water. He wet her parched lips but could not force any water down her.

Then the grandfather realized that Willow Wand was indeed going through the fast, and that nature was confirming in her what Whispering Birch had told him on her death bed. Suddenly her breasts began to heave and Willow Wand stood up. She struck a large rock which curved out ward and commanded, "WATER!"

Soon Aikie-wai-sie heard the sounds of water running from the girls fingers. Her pains fled from her in an instant, her health was back. Willow Wand and her grandfather drank to their fullness.

Once the fast was over the grandfather told Willow Wand the story of her miraculous power. She was but one in a long line of women who had been possessors of the power. As he spoke, Willow Wand thought she heard another voice telling her to watch for danger was near. Aikie-wai-sie was tired from relating the many tales to her and he quickly fell into a deep sleep. Willow Wand posted herself next to him as guard to watch over him during the night.

As night fell Willow Wand watched the eerie red light emanate from the Devil's Cave. She listened and trembled as there came the shrieks of men whom the Red Geebis were torturing. The sound of their suffering filled Willow Wand's heart with an ache.

The bear snuggled close to Willow Wand and the girl sensed that the bear too felt sorrow for the unfortunate sufferers. She wondered if this bear were not a person, who, like her grandfather had once been, was now bewitched by the evil one.

With the night came a storm which increased as the hours wore on. Haggard clouds swirled overhead, as birds of evil omen circled. The lightning flashed with great intensity, the wind roared and the rain pelted the earth as though with great anger.

In this tempest Willow Wand's mind returned to those suffering in the cave. She wondered if there were not some way her special gift could be used to help them. She stared from her resting place to that cave of horrors and saw a vision which was terrible for her to comprehend: being lead into the cave was her lover Kewe-naw. He was placed before a central fire.

Willow Wand cried out with sorrow. Her grandfather awoke and was himself overcome with grief when she told him what she had seen. His fear for the girl and for himself increased greatly until the bear whispered in his ear to watch and to not be afraid.

Aikie-wai-sei then turned to Willow Wand and spoke, "The spirit of your mother resides in the bear. Don't be afraid. When the spirits of the good abide no harm will come."

Willow Wand tried to control her fear. She threw herself upon the great shaggy beast in order to gain strength from her mother's spirit which resided therein. Yet her eyes were still transfixed as she watched the horror which the cannibal demons were acting out in tune to the orders of their elder.

Willow Wand observed many young men from her own tribe who had been given up as dead. Now they were being brought in one at a time and were offered as an appeasement to the wicked manitous. The evil spirits were ready to help in the evil doing and nightly fed on the quivering flesh of the brave young warriors.

The young girl leapt to her feet. She was determined to attempt a rescue before the firm flesh of her lover twisted its way through the insides of the evil one. Her movement was noticed by the Red Geebis, they knew that she was the "Wand of Power" which their demonic chief longed to possess. He commanded that the horrible ceremonies stop until he captured the Wand and returned to the odorous cave with his prize.

In all the commotion Kewe-naw was left standing near the edge of the entrance of the cave. From his vantage point he observed Willow Wand, her grandfather and the she-bear on the ledge. He could also see the evil chief near them and readying himself to take the Wand as his captive. To the rear, in the cave, Kewenaw could hear the babblings and the demonic laughs of glee from the contemptible monsters spawned by the very breath of hell. The creatures were unhappy as their feasting on smoking human flesh had been interrupted.

The spirit of Whispering Birch dwelling in the bear was delighted at the unselfish heroism which her daughter possessed. She whispered in her spirit voice to Aikie-wai-sie to not be afraid, because if the girl followed the promptings of nature all would be well.

As Willow Wand observed the evil one making himself ready for her capture she laughed scornfully at the hideous Geebi. Her laughter resounded as thousands of musical echoes among the melancholy rocks and hills of the island. As all this transpired the bear slipped from sight, feeling confident that all would be well for Willow Wand and those she loved.

Aikie-wai-sie was quite disturbed by the bear vanishing. Willow Wand stood strong and told him that fear was not necessary as her mother spirit was mingling with her own. Then she declared that Kewe-naw would be rescued and the sun would shine on the new day with happiness.

The demon chief had disguised himself as a warrior who Willow Wand's people recognized as being particularly blood thirsty. It was his intent to scare Aikie-wai-sie into accepting him as a son-in-law for he believed that the girl would not use her magic against him.

The disguise was well conceived, however, Willow Wand could see right through the facade. With great scorn she told him to begone. Her rejection made the foul creature writhe with anger. Forgetting his act he leapt from his secure place behind some rocks and attempted to seize Willow Wand. The magical girl, having seen his act, sprung at him and with a blow of her hand came such a gush of water that it sent him reeling backward. The evil chief fell, shrieking, into the Dead Hole. The fires which burned brightly in the cave became drenched with the healing waters, and Kewenaw began to have hope that his life might be spared.

The Okies and the Red Spirits vowed to rekindle the flames just as soon as they patched up the holes above. The water, they believed would make the roasting pit hotter than ever. But Kewenaw believed his deliverance was at hand. He looked about, and Willow Wand seeing his need waved toward him a rainbow colored mist which formed a bridge. He crossed the bridge safely to the ledge where he found Willow Wand reclining against Aikie-wai-sie, both sound asleep as though nothing had happened.

Kewenaw sat down beside the couple to await their awakening. Across the eastern sky streaks of red hues signaled the arrival of dawn. Willow Wand awoke and signaled her lover to silence. She took her grandfathers knife from her grandfather's belt and cut the thongs which secured Kewe-naw's strong arms. She prepared a pipe for him to smoke that he might again know the earthly pleasures he had been deprived of during his capture by the Red Geebis.

The joy they felt at being together again needed not to be expressed in words. It was an unspoken understanding between the lovers.

Throughout the day the grandfather slept, Kewe-naw smoked the stone pipe and Willow Wand worked clearing the cave of its remaining horrors. Single handed she flung the shrieking demons into the Lake Huron and she completely extinguished their smoldering fires. When she finished her choir and returned to the ledge it was very late.

As the hours wore on Aikie-wai-sie woke from his sound slumber. His heart was filled with joy to see the two lovers embraced. His blessing was delivered to the young couple and then he joined their hands in marriage.

Kewe-naw explained to them the plight he had come through. An evil spell had come upon him. When the fishing season had come to an end, he had set out for the island so that he could join his tribe before they left for the winter. A sudden storm came up on the lake and his canoe tipped over, sinking to the bottom as though it were made of lead. Kewe-naw thought that he would follow suit as swimming was very difficult in such a raging squall. There had appeared before him a pair of moccasins floating on the crests of the waves. Kewe-naw put his feet into them only to find them flashing with lightening. They whisked him with great swiftness to the Devil's Cave.

In turn Willow Wand told him of the gift she had discovered within herself. She told him how she drove the devils from the cave, and how she had commanded the mists to form the bridge on which he had escaped. She told how she had spent the day making the cave into a place she hoped would be a comfortable home.

The signal which Willow Wand had placed on the cliffs finally did its job. Fishermen came, and from them Kewe-naw purchased a canoe, and supplies which had been prepared for winter use.

The home was warm and comfortable. The winter passed by with the young couple having spent the first months of their marriage in happiness. When in the spring, the tribe returned, they found that Aikie-wai-sie was living a contented life with the young couple.

One early account concludes the story as follows, "When they were told that Willow Wand had worked all the changes by a powerful magic which she possessed, they easily believed it, and said that nothing but magic could banish evil spirits and make a happy home out of what was once a place of torment—the Devil's Kitchen. When the young couple showed them the whirling pool which lay between the Island of the Round Game and their own, and they saw the bodies of the demons rise to the surface of the water in proof of what Willow Wand's power had done, they were at once accepted as prophets whose medicine was good."

Not far from Devil's Kitchen is another spot known as Devil's Lake. These lands and waters were infested with fearsome creatures and probably one of the most fearsome of all was the manitou who lived in this former lake.

As the story goes, near the Devil's Kitchen, also known as the Cave of the Red Geebis, there was at one time a bottomless lake. The waters were inhabited by a very evil manitou. There is a cold water that still drips down from the rocks, and legend has it that this water once served the Geebis in the making of their human flesh stews.

In ancient times when the lake was still filled with water, the people were quite fearful of going to the lake because of the malignant manitou. He was a wily one! He could sings songs so soft and sweet, melodies that would lure unsuspecting children to his home—and they never returned.

Little Rail's wife was very lovely, and she was young. It happened that one evening she went to swim in the "musical waters." She did not have a dread of the place for she was not from her husband's tribe and she did not know of the stories concerning Devil's Lake.

It was a typical northeast Michigan summers eve. The air was sultry, humid and was rich with the pungent odors of the pine forest. Thunder heads rolled above and threatened of an impending storm. The young woman was a very fine swimmer and so the choppy waters did not hold fear for her. Standing by the reflective pool she removed her beautiful feathered garment. Naked, she stepped slowly into the dark waters.

The soft moss and mud felt good against her feet. The odorous branches of the trees growing on the shore fanned the spicy air around her.

All of nature was in wonderment at her beauty. The swallows stopped their nest building to observe the wonderful human as she bathed. But suddenly the birds sought shelter, as did all the other forest creatures. The young woman sensed danger as a stormy gust swept across the lake.

Lightening flashed from the ominous clouds as the thunder pealed heavily. Hoping that she might reach her lodge before the rain broke, she dashed from the water and quickly dressed in her feathered garb.

Then came a dire revelation as the lightening flashed before her. There was a terrible form moving towards her from the lake. As one of the sources puts it, "The lake no longer gave forth delicious music, but howled and raged in the gathering gloom, its deep bosom shaking, its writhing wavelips sending most awful and gruesome shrieks after the monster Geebis, who was about to land upon the beach at her feet. She turned to fly from the place, but she could move neither hand nor foot—she was fixed to the spot."

The demon which approached her was a beast man, but more beast than man. It head and face was that of a human, but it was ornamented by a pair of cow's horns; its body was like an ox except that from its body grew long stiff hairs; Its hoofs were cloven, but the arms and hands were like those of a muscular man.

Do you believe that all things have an aura? What do you make of this one? It is said that a peculiar bluish light enveloped the monster, and cast its light for many feet all around the beast.

The hideous devil's designs can only be imagined as he caught the young woman in his powerful arms. He bellowed with demonic laughter as he stripped off her garment of feathers, taking particular delight in despoiling each and every one. He next commanded that from this day hence she would serve only him.

The young woman was terribly afraid. She commended herself heart and mind to the Great Spirit—fearing for her life. She hoped that if her life were to be given that it might somehow benefit her loved ones.

The young girl's agony was multiplied as she saw her husband approaching. First she could see him clearly, then darkly as the light emanating from the beast had a pulsating quality. She was powerless to warn Little Rail of his impending danger.

As Little Rail saw his bride in the grasp of the horrible Geebis, he flew into a rage and leapt upon the beast in an effort to secure her release. He fought hard with tremendous blows being delivered from his powerful arms, but the efforts were fruitless. The fight was against spiritual powers and Little Rail's attempts were useless when pitted against these odds.

The handsome young brave pleaded with his wife to make her escape and to take flight to the sanctified ground where the evil one would dare not tread. But then he caught a glimpse of it in her eyes, she was under the evil spell of the Geebis and he had not until that moment realized it.

The Geebis was infuriated by the attempted rescue. Shrieking with rage he threatened the life of his captive, but instead further enhanced Little Rail's suffering by finishing his spell on the bride. He commanded that she should dance for him, and he told Little Rail when she had finished that he would take her to her new home at the bottom of the lake.

She began to dance before the horrible manitou. Her will was completely under his control and she could not help but do as he commanded. But by dancing she was breaking the laws of her people, as to them dance was for certain special times and seasons. The manitou was displeased with her efforts and at length to shorten the misery of Little Rail his bride was allowed to do the death dance. She felt certain her own doom was near by doing the unholy dance.

As she carefully placed her steps the evil manitou watched with pleasure. Surely the evil one took pleasure at Little Rail's agony. His heart ached and tears streamed from his eyes. He pleaded in vain for the life of his bride. But the evil one only laughed.

At last the Geebis told Little Rail that he would watch his wife descend into the bottom of the lake. He cruelly added that he would not be united with the lovely young woman until the lake had become dry land.

With a powerful gesture the Geebis thrust Little Rail's bride into the deep water. His cruelty knew no bounds. He stood his place for hours on the shore casting stones at the young woman so that she could not rise. Then in one last act of cruel torture he turned to Little Rail who was setting with his eyes covered so as to hide the tears.

With one twist of his strong bony fingers, the Geebis snapped Little Rails back so that from that day on he became a hunch-back.

Little Rail bore his pain like a true brave. He made a vow that no matter how long it took, he would be true to his bride. To hasten the day of their reunion Little Rail spent much time throwing stones into the pond in an attempt to fill it up. Once this was done, Little Rail believed his wife would be restored to him, as a manitou, good or evil, never went back on its word.

Not satisfied with his own work, Little Rail enlisted the aid of anyone he could find who was sympathetic to his cause. It soon became customary to do penance by casting stones into the waters. Small stones were used as an appeasement for small offenses, and large boulders for larger offenses. An additional stone was cast in each time to hasten the rejoining of the two souls.

This custom spread far and wide and entire tribes would come to the Devil's Lake to cast stones in for deliverance from sins they had committed.

It is told that on still nights the voice of the evil manitou could be heard laughing at the hard toil of the husband. Sometimes the demon became so obnoxious that it was necessary for a shaman to quiet the damming spirit with sacred incantations.

But nowadays the voice of the evil manitou is silent. The great lake of his abode is now filled up, and one can assume that as per his promise, Little Rail and his bride are reunited. But Little Rail would never regain his handsome figure, he would always be a broken back little duck.

Bibliography

The Tree That Never Dies: Oral History of the Michigan Indian edited by Pamela J. Dobson—Grand Rapids Public Library/1978

The Hiawatha Legends by Henry R. Schoolcraft—J.B. Lippincott & Co.,/1856

The Chippewa Village by W. Vernon Kinietz—Cranbrook Institute of Science/1947.

Kitchi-Gami by J.G. Kohl—Ross and Haines/1956

The First People of Michigan by W.B. Hinsdale—Ann Arbor Press/1930

Lame Deer Seeker of Visions by John (Fire) Lame Deer and Richard Erdoes—Simon & Schuster/1972

Mystic Warriors of the Plains by Thomas E. Mails—Doubleday & Co./1972

Indian Rock Paintings of the Great Lakes by Selwyn Dewdrey and Kenneth E. Kidd—University of Toronto Press/1973

The Search For Lost America by Salvatoe Michael Trento—Contemporary Books/1978

The Chippewas of the Lake Superior by Edmund Jefferson Danziger Jr.,—University of Oklahoma Press/1978

Warpath by Stanley Vestal—Houghton Mifflin & Co./1934

The Indians Secret World by Robert Hofsinde (Gray Wolf)—William Morris & Co./1955

The Jesuit Relations edited by Edna Kenton—Vanguard Press/1954

Indians of the Western Great Lakes by W. Vernon Kinietz—Ann Arbor Paperbacks/1965.

Bloodstoppers & Bearwalkers By Richard M. Dorson—Harvard University Press/1952

"Mock-wa-mosa: The Bearwalker Cult" by Dennis Michael Morrison *Indian Artifacts Magazine*, Volume 9 Issue 3/Summer 1990.

God's Frozen Children by Harold McCracken—Doubleday, Doran & Co.,/1930

The Eskimo by Edward Moffat Weyer—Yale University Press/1932

"Naub-cow-zo-win Discs From Northern Michigan" by Charles Cleland, Richard Clute and Robert E. Haltiner—*Midcontinental Journal of Archaeology*, Volume 9 Issue 2/1984

"The Shaking Tent Rite Among the Montagnais of James Bay" by Regina Flanerry—*Catholic Anthropological Conference*, Volume 12/1939

The American Indian by Henry R. Schoolcraft—Wanzer, Foot & Co.,/1851

"The Ches-a-kee Men" By Jerry Wagner—Unpublished paper in the authors private collection.

"Instructions for the Amateur Archaeologist" by Dennis Michael Morrison—*Western & Eastern Treasures*, Volume 24/March 1990.

"Mystery of the Possessed Indian Talisman" By Dennis Michael Morrison—*Inner Light* #19.

"Old Van Etten Creek: A Prehistoric Village In Northeast Michigan" by Dennis Michael Morrison—*Heritage*, Volume 6 Issue 2/February 1989.

"Pottery Types of Oscoda, Michigan" by Dennis Michael Morrison—*Indian Artifacts Magazine*, Volume 3 Issue 2/Spring 1989.

"Prehistoric Pipes In Northeast Michigan" by Dennis Michael Morrison—*Indian Artifacts Magazine*, Volume 10 Issue 3/Summer 1991.

"Historical Tales of the Huron Shore Region" by R.E. Prescott—*Alcona County Herald*/1934.

Celebrate The Legendary Ways of the Shamans

and Experience the Supernatural Powers of Native Indian Prophecy, Mysticism & Spirituality

Here are four remarkable works and one audio cassette tape that will lead you on a personal vision quest. Find out why thousands of metaphysical students are turning to the "Good Red Road" and the ways of the medicine men and tribal chiefs for inner perfection and personal guidance.

#1
MYSTICAL LEGENDS OF THE SHAMANS
by Brad and Sherry Steiger

Here are the little known legends involving the spiritual and mystical as well as psychic experiences of the North American Indians—the medicine men, chiefs and shamans of various tribes. A rare collection of Amerindian legends that have been repeated by generations of shamans employing the oral tradition of telling enchanting tales around the evening campfires. The incredible power of these legends remains undimmed by the passage of time, and their applications of vital truths for modern men and women becoming increasingly self-evident. Among the mystic shamanistic legends are such tales as: • How the spirits of the four winds came to be. • When the animals ruled the Earth mother. • The origin of the races. • The first battle between good and evil. • Entering the land of shadows. • Mysterious visitors to our world. • The ghostly canoe. • The daughter of the evening star descends to take a husband • Spirit beings of thunder and lightning, and many, many more.

There is also a special section: STARS: GUARDIANS OF THE NIGHT—on Amerindian cosmology; revelations of things to come in the chapter, THE EARTH MOTHER AND PROPHECY; sacred talismans that can be put to personal work for you in the section AMERICAN INDIAN POWER SYMBOLS, and finally a timely photographic portfolio of the great medicine men and chiefs of our time.

This beautiful, coffee table-sized book, contains 100 pages and comes complete with a glorious air-brushed cover painted by native American artist Timoteo Ikoshy Montoya. To order simply circle #1 in the order coupon—$12.95.

#2
THE AMERICAN INDIAN UFO-STARSEED CONNECTION
Edited and annotated by Timothy Green Beckley

Do the various Amerindian tribes know a lot more about space visitors than the rest of us—including, perhaps, even the United States government?

With chapters by some of the most astute metaphysical writers, such as Brad Steiger, Diane Tessman, David Jungclause and Chris Franz, this book delves into the traumatic "Last Days" that many sensitives say are not far off and the "feeling" that the Indians may help lead us to a safe New World based upon their connection with beings from other realms and worlds.

Explored are striking revelations concerning the famous Hopi Prophecies and a mysterious artifact unearthed at the site of a newly discovered pyramid that suggests that the end of the current cycle of Mother Earth is about to come to an end, and that something more "wonderful" will replace it as we are pulled brother with brother toward the climax of an era.

Learn the significance of the Kachina spirits of the sky and when they are to return; what meaning the creature known as Bigfoot has in relationship to the Indian tribes; why UFOs are so frequently seen—even today—over the

various reservations. Find out what the mysterious "Star symbol" of the UFO-nauts means in the context of the sacred Medicine Wheel, and how the dreams that many of us are now having may turn out to be very prophetic.

This is a large sized book containing over 100 pages. When released in December it will retail for $14.95. Order now at the special pre-publication price by circling #2 on the order coupon—$12.95.

#3
AMERICAN INDIAN CEREMONIES—
A PRACTICAL GUIDE TO THE MEDICINE PATH
by Medicine Hawk and Gray Cat

Medicine Hawk (Council Chief, the Shadowlight Medicine Clan) and Gray Cat (editor, the *Crone Papers*) present dozens of practical and concise ceremonies enabling the reader to practice the concepts of the Sacred Pipe and the Medicine Wheel, regardless of their heritage and in a manner that is true to the environment of our living Earth.

Learn to master the ancient and sacred ways that can now be passed to the Truth Seeker as we enter a New Age of Spiritual Enlightenment. Here are all the powers and tools YOU will ever need to Walk the Good Red Road.

Discusses in detail the construction of the Medicine Wheel, the true role of the Vision Quest, the use of the Sacred Pipe, the relationship of the Sweat Lodge, the important of the Animal and plant kingdoms, as well as the magick in pictographs and symbols.

This volume contains 150 8½x11 pages and is attractively illustrated with photos, graphs and charts. Circle number 3 on the order form—$14.95.

#4
AMERICAN INDIAN MAGIC—
SACRED POW WOWS & HOPI PROPHECIES
by Brad Steiger

Through a few simple techniques the reader will learn how to make American Indian Magic work for YOU! Over the centuries, the native American priests have practiced a system of magic so powerful that it enables them to control the winds and the weather, to foresee coming events, and sometimes even to change the future. They have always possessed the ability to heal the sick, to walk over burning coals, to read minds, to send and receive telepathic thoughts, to communicate with the dead, speak to animals, and to control others at a distance. This book is a practical guide which teaches, among other things, the American Indian's way to perfection, telling the reader how to: • Hold your own "Vision Quest." • Communicate with spirits and angels and get them to assist you in all that you desire. • Take control of every situation and through a formal agreement with the forces of nature, receive incredible benefits that can turn your life around for the better.

Circle #4 and find out how Indian Magic can be of service to you!—$12.95.

#5
60 MINUTE AUDIO CASSETTE
INDIAN MEDICINE WHEEL
with Brad Steiger

Journey to dimensions never before experienced with this Altered States Awareness cassette tape. Hold your own Vision Quest, prepare your own Medicine Bag of sacred and highly charged objects. Communicate with spirits of the Earth and Sky. Many tribes believe that the Medicine Wheel can cure the sick, ward off evil and bring great blessings. Now the author of **AMERICAN INDIAN MAGIC** leads you through various meditations complete with authentic Indian prayers and chants.

Circle number 5 for this outstanding audio cassette tape—$9.95.